LEAVING A LEGACY FOR THE SUCCEEDING GENERATION

JOHNSON F. ODESOLA

authorHOUSE®

AuthorHouse™
1663 Liberty Drive
Bloomington, IN 47403
www.authorhouse.com
Phone: 1 (800) 839-8640

Published by AuthorHouse 12/19/2019

ISBN: 978-1-7283-3991-7 (sc)
ISBN: 978-1-7283-3990-0 (e)

Print information available on the last page.

Scripture taken from The Holy Bible, King James Version. Public Domain

This book is printed on acid-free paper.

CONTENTS

ACKNOWLEDGEMENT

I give all Glory, praise and adoration to God, the Father, Jesus my Saviour and the Holy Spirit the director of my life affairs, programmes and inspiration. My sincere appreciation to 'Bisi, my darling wife, for her unflinching support and encouragement and to my home church members, Titillate, Uche and Enoch. Special thanks to my spiritual parents, Daddy and Mummy E A Adeboye. They are both my coaches on the way to greatness

I am indebted to Pastor and Pastor (Mrs) E A Odeyemi, my uncle and friend, Bishop Joe Imakando, Bishop Tayo Odunuga, Bishop Paul Aigboje, Rev Sam O Igbari, Professor Gordon Beck, Pastor Isaac Oyebanji, Rev Colin Megaw, Paul Johnston, Dough Lago, Dr Graham Cheesman, Rev Drew Gibson, All BBC Staff, Bill Branan Jnr., Biodun Idiagbon, Deaconess Oyedepo, Japheth Njovu, Pastor Olotu, Pastor Amoni, Pastor & Pastor (Mrs) Dele Olowu, Pastor Femi Popoola, Pastor Adeniyi Daniel, Pastor Charles Achonwa, Rev Moses Aransiola, Pastor Joe Olaiya, Pastor and Mrs Andrew Adeleke, Pastor Abraham Adeniji, Pastor and Pastor and Mrs Bamigbade, Pastor Akhazema, Pastor Bolarinwa, the Oyedumades, the Makindes, the Olatunyas, Olaniyan Timothy a friend indeed both when present and absent. Also I am thankful to various authors from whose works had been quoted at various stages and those whose facility had contributed towards my thought on this book.

I appreciate the contribution of my colleagues for their support and Godly efforts, which was the basic mover of this work. They include Pastors Gboyega & Shade Kalejaiye, John Sumonu, Peter & Sola Amenkeinah, Dele Balogun, Seyi & Kemi Oladosu, Yombo King, Pastor Oyedele, the Kapulus, Richard Adeboye, Jide Akiode, Lekan Aruna, Simanga Moyo, Olu Obanure, Toyin Olugbemi, Prince Obasi-Ike, Esther Obasi-Ike,

Segun & Bimpe Ogunmodede, Eunice Sanya, Bayo Adewole, Dr & Pastor Oshinfade, Pastor & Dr Oyedunmade, Clement Osho, Pastos & Mrs Oladoye, 'Demola Farinu, Pastor Olojo, Joseph & Christie Obayemi, Ayo Obafemi, Remi Akintunde, Pastor Akande, Pastor Adetayo, Kola and Sola Oworu, Julius Olalekan, David Omunagbe, Ola Adejubee, Moronike Olla, Kayode Oladunjoye, Mary Wanayo, Segun Aladeniyi, Ibukun Aderibigbe, Funke Masondo, Peter Olawale, Chibose Amusaa, Stephen Friday, Gbenga Ilesanmi, Johnson Fenibo, Tunde Oginni, John Mbayo, Elijah Lisoyi, Fenibo Johnson, 'Demi & Tayo Fijabi, Funke Masondo, Yemi Ajiboye, Pastor Adedoyin, Muyiwa Fakunle, Tunji Olasunkanmi, Bode & Bukky Odesola, Yemi Philips, Sam Ore, Toyin Olaoye, Apostle Kamulile Phiri, Bishop Jericho, Mark Nyasulu, Deacon Venom, the Femi & Wumi Bankole and others.

Furthermore I cannot forget all my leaders in RCCG, CRM and also the past and present members of RCF in all the campuses of higher institutions & RCCF in all States for direct and indirect contribution. My special thanks to Pastor Biodun & Yemi Oluwalabu, Wole, Doja & Segun Olatunya, All members of the Africa Missions UK Chapter, the members of staff of SA I Secretariat of R.C.C.G. – Elias Musonda, Dr Kola & Yemisi Odubote, Raphael Matola, Remmy Chikumbi and others.

Thank you all may God bless you.

Author's address
Johnson F Odesola
WINGS ZAMBIA
91a Mutandwa Road (Roma) P O Box RW 50838
Lusaka ZAMBIA
Tel/Fax: +260-1-293652 Cell: 97-749354 and 95-749354

CHAPTER 1

YOUR EXALTATION IS DETERMINED BY YOUR MOTIVATION

You are the principal architect of your destiny. You are a direct product of whatever you become in life.

Your motivation is not the function of chance; it is an effort of your personal input; your input in life determines your output.

The major determinant of your destiny is you. Although you can be encouraged or stirred up by others, you have the unreserved power to dictate your future. Many may look down on you, don't look down on yourself.

If you cannot find anyone to tell you that you can make it to your destiny, tell yourself you will make it to the top. If you refuse to be defeated inside, no outside force will defeat you.

No force is capable of stopping you if you refuse to stop yourself. Every obstacles and opposition are raw materials to develop your achievements muscle.

Paul, an apostle of the Lord motivated himself; he left the footprints on the sand of time. Read what he said in Phil 3:13 -14:

> *Brethren, I count not myself to have apprehended: but this one thing I do, forgetting those things which are behind, and reaching forth unto those things which are before, I press toward the mark for the prize of the high calling of God in Christ Jesus.*

He was consciously motivated to success. History will not forget him in a hurry. Be awake to your success. Launch yourself into the world of achievement by motivating yourself.

The match is still on. If you refuse to blow the final whistle on yourself no one will, determine to win the match. The panel of judges are on your side.

Life is a race, it is not the starting point that determines the winner but the finishing point, you must make it to the finishing point. Refuse to stop yourself, you must make it to success, it's your time and your turn for success.

Many who are successful today didn't have it easy at the beginning, things were tight and tough but they refuse to yield to *Your exaltation is determined by your motivation* circumstances and situations and later success smiled at them. It takes you holding on doggedly before you can win a price. Motivate yourself never to accept defeat.

"A future that cannot be pictured cannot be earned".

Here is a story of a man who pictured his future and motivated himself to it.
- He lost his job in 1832.
- He was elected into the legislature in 1834.
- He suffered the death of his sweetheart in 1834.
- He was defeated for speaker of the state legislature in 1848.
- He was rejected for the position of land office in 1845.
- He was defeated for the senate in 1854.
- He was defeated for the nomination for Vice–President of the United States in 1856.
- He was again defeated for the Senate in 1858.
- He was elected President of the United States in 1860.

The name of this man is Abraham Lincoln, can you imagine the harassment of failure on him before success blew out his failure.

"Men of recognition are not recorder of history but rather greater of history".

It is not how many times you have failed that matters; it is the ability to turn your failure to success that counts. Why should you give up because you have failed a couple of times? Do not give up that venture that seems not to be yielding a desired result, motivate yourself in the Lord. Apply a different strategy and win.

You cannot afford to live and die a failure because you are not created to be a failure. Don't give up your pursuit, move on and win. Your ability to motivate yourself determines your winning level. You do not become a failure by failing but you become a failure by giving up. Until a man decides not to try again he is still a prospective winner.

Don't lose your position to test and trial; do not relinquish your championship to little obstacles. Don't let go the fame and reward of your celebrity to stumbling block. Refuse to join the group of the disgruntled and discontented.

In your chosen profession you must be a champion; obstacles should not stop you. No athlete wins a prize that stopped in the middle of the race. It is too costly for you to stop now; there is a prize ahead that you must win.

One of my previous books titled *"Candidate for the Throne"* Three classes of people were identified thus:

Garbage Class: People without impact, their existence is of no benefits to anyone; neither the World; they constituted part of the problem in our generation.

Grasshopper Class: People existing but not living. They are quick to identify good things, but they never get to possess it.

Giant Class: They are people of impact; they turn obstacles to miracles, trials to triumph, test to testimony, frustration to fruition and failure to fullness.

Which of this class are you? To join the giant class you must be ready to shun every unprogressive news, be ready for battle, prepare to turn stumbling blocks to stepping stone; move on and win go ahead and make impact. You can do it; nothing can stop you except you stop yourself. The Heroes of faith did it; the same strength is available to you.

Hebrew 11: 33 – 34 said that;

> *Who through faith subdued kingdoms, wrought righteousness, obtained promises, stopped the mouths of lions, quenched the violence of fire, escaped the edge of the sword, out of weakness were made strong, waxed valiant in fight, turned to flight the armies of the aliens.*

You are the major determinant of your destiny. Nobody is to be blamed if you fail. Self-motivation is the energy anchor that holds the key of achievement. Success is not cheap; it is obtained through the energy of self-motivation.

For your goals to be achieved you don't need to retire but re-fire. Success is for few who refuse to retire but re-fire when their desire seems to expire.

When your world tears apart, when your effort to success seems abortive, when things refuse to go the way you have been expecting, all you need is to persevere, success is closer to you than you think or imagine. The road to success is full of stumbling blocks but through self- motivation and persistence you can turn your stumbling blocks into stepping stones.

Glenn Cunmigham was burnt so horribly as a boy that his legs were expected to be amputated. They told him that he would not walk again but he did not give up. He disciplined himself in steel wheel, he did a lot of exercise, he motivated himself; he later became one of the world's greatest distance runners.

When you lack self-motivation; you lack what it takes to make a good and excellent life. Achievement is for few who, in spite of all odds, they encourage themselves to become what they are destined to be

CHAPTER 2

LIFE CYCLONE

I think that there isn't anyone who could deny the fact that human beings are complex creatures, with much more to them than what meets the eye. We feel anger, love, sympathy, frustration, hurt and a dozen other emotions throughout our lives.

Life moves at a whirlwind pace, constantly shifting us from one circumstance to another, sometimes forcing us from one emotion to the next within moments. Is it any wonder, then, that most of us have experienced deep sadness or depression? Is it any wonder that we sometimes feel so very out of control of own lives?

Sometimes during the trials of my life, I have often wondered, *"how do others do it? How does everyone else find the strength to crawl out of bed one more day?"* It used to seem mind boggling to me and extremely incomprehensible. But then finally, I discovered the answer.

God placed us on this hectic earth that sometimes seems out of control but I couldn't believe that the loving, kind and merciful God I had been taught to believe in would place us on this out of control earth without giving us gifts: tools, to help us find the eye of life's storm.

> *When I consider thy heavens, the work of thy fingers, the moon and the stars, which thou hast ordained; What is man, that thou art mindful of him? And the son of man, that thou visitest him? For thou hast made him a little lower than the angels, and hast crowned him with glory and honour. Thou madest him to have dominion over the works of thy hands; thou hast put all things under his feet:* (Psalms 8:3-6)

I was right. He *has* given each of us several different weapons to help control our lives. One of the best weapons He's given us is our talent, our self-expression. Mine happens to be preaching, motivating, writing etc while that of my wife is impacting children. Others find theirs in singing or acting or sports or any number of things.

There are as many different forms of self-expression, talent, as there are people but the point is that we all have one. If we can only look within ourselves and discover our talents, then we can use them to help us feel better whenever the going gets tough. Whenever I feel overwhelmed, for instance, I pull out my pen and within moments, literally, I'm taken away to an imaginary world of writing and everything is within my grasp once more. Not only does using our talents help us feel better about the situation, it helps us feel better about ourselves. Wouldn't you agree that just having good self-esteem often helps us conquer depression?

But God is full of grace and understanding: He realized that some people may never find their talent or be able to learn to use it instead of more unhealthy ways to live, so He provided another outlet: words. Though sometimes used in anger that can be weapons of pain and degradation, words are, I believe, one of healing's most remarkable assets. Just talking about our lives and the many different emotions we have helps so much. It gives us a sense of not being alone, and the knowledge that another human being cares enough to listen to us talk about those things and to understand could provide immense relief. Sometimes, it's even harder to learn to use words for our benefit as part of the comforting and healing process, but when we do, I believe, it is one of the most effective.

After all, God created Eve because Adam was lonely and didn't have anyone to talk to about the challenges of living in an out of control world or to share its joys. Since the beginning of creation then, conversation has been one of man's most valuable and powerful tools.

God, though, is all-knowing and He knew that the many millions of people He would create would all have different personalities. Some would find peace and happiness with self- expression, while others would find it with the communicative ability of words. But what about the rest of the people? And what about those times when self-expression and conversation aren't enough even for those who know how to appreciate and use them? What then? Were humans meant to merely suffer?

No.

For those people, and those times, God provided the most powerful tool of all and often the most effective, for any situation. Being able to actually talk to God Himself is an experience that can give the soul its greatest control, its greatest peace. Yes, this life is a whirlwind but talking to the One who created it can help restore order to it, and help us through life's more difficult moments. I believe that each and every day is filled with as many good things as bad things. Romans 8:28:

> *And we know that all things work together for good to them that love God, to them who are the called according to his purpose.*

The key, though, is to open our eyes and discover the small acts of kindness given to us by strangers and friends alike. When we have control and order in our lives and when we stand in the middle of happiness' light then it's easier to see those daily good events. And though it's hard sometimes, when we use those gifts God has given us: self-expression, conversation and prayer, to combat the more confusing and difficult moments, then we are more quick to find, and appreciate, the happiness that we were all meant to find.

CHAPTER 3

YOUR CONFIDENCE CO-OPTED YOU FOR SUCCESS

The tool for the winners is confidence; it is the outstanding weapon for the champions.

It is indeed true that the battles of life are not won by struggle but by ability to approach situations with total confidence.

Confidence is the powerful medicine that has no side effects. It relaxes your muscles and makes man to produce at his best and to maximize his life.

You have unlimited power because the unlimited God lives in you. Be confident! You are unbeatable because the man of war dwells in you. You cannot be killed before your time because the Hands that hold the world are enwrapped around you. Loaded creative ideas are within you because you are an extension of the divine Omniscience. Greatness is in you! Healthy, Wisdom, Riches are in you, be confident of what is in you.

Do not stop yourself, hear what *Richard Devos* says: *The only thing that stands between a man and what he wants from life is often merely the will to try it and the confidence that it is possible!*

Have you ever watched wrestling match you will be puzzled with the way the wrestler boast and exert confidence before the fight with the opponent.

Most of the time the confidence exerted before the match always tells on their performance in the ring. That shows clearly that confidence is the vital tool to success.

You need to be rest assured that your tomorrow will be better than today, be assured that whatever you are passing through now is a stepping stone to your greatness. The world is a comedy to those that think, a tragedy to those that feel. The way you see things affect the way things goes. *Clement stone* said; *"There is little difference in people and that little difference makes a big difference"*. The little difference is attitude. The big difference is whether it is positive or negative. All the water in the world won't sink your boat if it does not get inside of you! Hebrews 10:35 says:

Cast not away therefore your confidence, which hath great recompense of reward.

Confidence has a great reward: It does not only make life great but highly rewarding.

A failure is not the one that attempts something worthwhile and not achieves it but the one for fear of failure did not try at all. Nothing will ever be attempted if all possible objections must first be overcome. Inculcate the habit of waking up a day and approaching the day with total confidence that you cannot fail.

Let your total confidence be exhibited in your daily activities. Be bold; be confident; this is the path to your greatness. Never forget that one does not get what he or she want in life, you can only get what you negotiate for. Sometimes the delays in your life today are allowed by God to remove evil and sorrow from your tomorrow.

When God measures man, He does not put the tape around the head, but around the heart. The consolation that tomorrow will be better should keep you going! Everyday of my life, I am inspired to brace up by the challenges of life, when they keep knocking. The Zeal to come out of a rough sport unscathed inspires me. Life on its own is not rosy. Life is all about how many hurdles you have to overcome, the challenges that you need to subdue.

All these life challenges should inspire you everyday. View life as a phase! A phase when after overcoming your hurdles in life, you will be recognized. There is a face in life that no matter what people will recognize you. I believe that "after a very rough road" with your confidence in God you will get there.

Do you know that there arose a King (Pharaoh) in Egypt that knew not Joseph? (Exodus 1:8). It was a rough and trouble phase for the Jews. But at the end, do they not come out of Egypt? You will also come out better, bigger and brighter.

Determine to be confident in the quiet phase of your life, because it is a preparation for your public phase. Nobody heard about Moses for 40 solid years, but he was very confidence in God those quite years.

Don't spend your quiet phase complaining neither regretting your background or wishing you were someone else. These are satanic lies to prolong that phase. Don't envy and be invidious of those who are being celebrated now - those who are in their public phase now! Be confidence that were you are, is a question of time.

Did not David kill the lion and the bear and yet he was not recognized? Did he murmur against his father Jesse? Did he abandon the sheep? Did he run around telling everyone what he had done or was doing? No he remained faithful and confident in God in the bush until his season came. Marie Curie says: *"Life is not easy for any of us: But what of that? We must above all, have confidence in ourselves".* We must believe that we are gifted for something and that this something at whatever cost, must be attained.

A true life story was told about a man who lost so much in business and when he got home in depression, self-pity and anger against God, he exclaimed: "My God I have lost all. I am finished" To his shock his four-year-old daughter walked up to him and said, Daddy but you still have me and mummy. You have not lost all. You have not lost us."

Those words hit the man like a thunder with a dose of confidence. He suddenly realized that no matter what has happened, a child of God cannot lose all. *"There is always something left for you to plan and begin again"* He realized that pains, trials, tragedies and life battles are only a passing phase. *"Then he leant the hidden secret of the ages that when there is God, there is hope".*

Please be patient and keep on holding on to your confidence in God. *Roger Banister* affirmed that: *The man who can drive himself further once the effort gets painful is the man who will win.* Where you have been is not half important to as to where you are going.

To expect life to be perfectly tailored to our perfection is to live a life of continual frustration.

Richard Nixon once said, even at the period when he was down and out. *"A man is not finished when he is defeated he is not finished, He is finished when he quits".*

There are no hopeless situations; there are only men who have grown hopeless about them. The education of the will is the object of our existence. For the resolute and determined, there is time and opportunity. Therefore do not cast away your confidence, which has recompense of great reward.

CHAPTER 4

STANDARD IS THE PLATFORM FOR STARDOM

If people do not know what you stand for they can draw you to anything. Anyone who refuses to stand for something always falls for anything. You are either known for your stand or become unknown.

If you want to make a mark and impact your generation then you must stand for something. If people did not know what you are standing for they will draw you away easily. No one can become somebody without standing for something. Check through the history of the people who have made it big in life. They all stood for something!

Three Hebrews set a standard and stood for God in their generation; (Daniel 3:16-20)

> *Shadrach, Meshach, and Abed-nego, answered and said to the king, O Nebuchadnezzar, we are not careful to answer thee in this matter.*
>
> *If it be so, our God whom we serve is able to deliver us from the burning fiery furnace, and he will deliver us out of thine hand, O king.*
>
> *But if not, be it known unto thee, O king, that we will not serve thy gods, nor worship the golden image, which thou hast set up. Then was Nebuchadnezzar full of fury, and the form of his visage was changed against Shadrach, Meshach, and*

Abed-nego: therefore he spake, and commanded that they should heat the furnace one seven times more than it was wont to be heated.

And he commanded the most mighty men that were in his army to bind Shadrach, Meshach, and Abed-nego, and to cast them into the burning fiery furnace.

These three boys stood firmly with their God and they were delivered from the furnace of the King. Make your stand known or you perpetually become unknown. If people don't know your stand, which may give rooms for many unimportant invitation; whereas if once they know what you stand for they will stop sending unimportant invitations to you.

There is an objective or purpose for living than wasting time in endless ceremonies and parties

My purpose in life is clear and I am success inclined, no one can call me to waste my time on an unproductive thing, even if you call me for such, you would be glad to miss me. It is time for you to stand for something so that you do not fall for many things. Let what you stand for be known to everybody. Choose a course you want to follow but make sure it is a productive course.

The organization I belong to stands for holiness, excellence and helping people to realize their destinies. We are committed to raising role models, sold out to the course of transforming followers into excellent leaders and raising people of purpose who will maximize their potential for the present and future generation with the sole aim of making it to heaven at last.

As you make up your mind to stand for something, you will definitely be criticized, envied and become an object of jealousy by many but that should not stop you from fulfilling your purpose and destiny. Have your own creed, focus and vision. I remember reading through the popular creed of John. D. Rockefeller Jnr. It goes thus:

"I believe in the supreme worth of the individual and in his right to life, liberty and pursuit of happiness. I believe that every right implies a responsibility; every possession, a duty, I believe in the dignity of labour - weather with head or hand;

that the world owes no manna living but that it owes every man an opportunity to make a living. I believe that truth and justice are fundamental to an enduring Social order. I believe in the sacredness of a promise; that a man's word should be as good as his bond: that character…not wealth and power or position is of supreme worth. I believe that love is the greatest thing in the world; that it alone can overcome hate, that light can and will always triumph over night. I believe that the rendering of useful service is the common duty of mankind and that only in the purifying fire of sacrifice is the dross of selfishness consumed. I believe in an all-wise and all- loving God and that the individual's highest fulfilment, greatest happiness and widest usefulness are to be found in living in harmony with his will."

Paul said *"I know in whom I believe and I am persuaded that He is able."* Believe in your God! Stand for your life goals! Be persuaded about them. Resist all arrows of discouragement! Stand for something! Write your own creed. One is not born to the world to do everything but to do something.

Things turn out the best for the people who make the best of the way things turn out.

Joseph stood for his dream though he was envied and became an object of jealousy by his brothers but that did not stop his dream, he stood by his dream and his dream came to pass.

In the house of Potiphar despite the pressure from Mrs. Potiphar, Joseph stood for righteousness and holiness. Mrs. Potiphar wanted to lure him into sin but he refused, he stood for his conviction; which is holiness, though he was thrown into the prison but he later became a Prime Minister of Egypt. (Genesis 39:7-9)

And it came to pass after these things, that his master's wife cast her eyes upon Joseph; and she said, Lie with me. But he refused, and said unto his master's wife, Behold, my master wotteth not what is with me in the house, and he hath committed all that he hath to my hand;

There is none greater in this house than I; neither hath he kept back anything from me but thee, because thou art his wife: how then can I do this great wickedness, and sin against God?

If Joseph had not stood for something he would have fallen for anything and his destiny would have been windswept. Every attempt to make it outside God always proves futile and unfruitful. If you do not secure God you cannot secure good.

Just as we discovered in the story of Joseph, every lasting success has its foundation in God. Every true greatness has its root in God. To refuse to place God were He belong is to make an cataleptic choice for failure.

No destiny becomes a reality outside God. God is the only one who makes dream come true. Until you make God your backbone you do not have a backbone. Watch it, every seemingly good success that does not have God as its foundation does not last. Every attempt to climb the ladder of success outside God always leads to regret and sorrow. To refuse to acknowledge God is to end up in the ditch. God is the brain behind true success. Jeremiah 17:7 says:

Blessed is the man that trusteth in the LORD, and whose hope the LORD isz

God is the only one who can take you to the peak. If you have lost every- thing in life except God, you have got enough to start all over again.

All that your destiny will ever require is in God. If you can place God where he belongs, then your destiny becomes tangible.

The way to secure God is to make Him first in all things, acknowledge Him in all your ways, let Him be number one in your life, like what He likes and hate what He hates, that is the foundation of uncommon success.

Watch it, every success outside God is like building a house without foundation, which definitely cannot stand. Go for God and good will automatically follow you (Proverbs 3:5 -6)

Trust in the LORD with all thine heart; and
lean not unto thine own understanding.
In all thy ways acknowledge him, and he shall direct thy paths.

Stand up for integrity; intelligence can take a man to the top but only integrity can retain him there Integrity is the path to a lasting throne.

Nothing works when integrity is at stake. Integrity is a force that makes success a reality. Integrity is superior to riches, fame, background and beauty. When a man loses integrity he automatically loses the power that can retain him at the top. (Ecclesiastes 7:1):

> *A good name is better than precious ointment; and the day of death than the day of one's birth.*

It is good to be rich but it is better to have a good name. It is good to be intelligent but it is better to have a good name.

Having a good name means being a person of integrity; a person that can be believed and trusted, a person who stands for truth and holiness, a person who always does things in the right way.

What are you standing for? Are you a man/woman of integrity? Do you stand for righteousness? Are you straight forward in all your ways? Do people really believe you? Can you be trusted?

Until the issue of integrity is settled, destiny is at stake. Whatever can make a man to lie to get money has brought his destiny into stagnancy.

If you can stand for integrity every good thing will stand in favour. Integrity outlives people who live in it, after they have gone they cannot be forgotten. The world today is in a dire need of people of integrity, people who will stand for nothing but righteousness and holiness in all ramifications, people whose yes will be yes and no will be no. If a man can pass the test of integrity he will definitely enter into distinction.

Determine to be a man/woman of integrity for the rest of your life. Horace Mann says:

> *"Keep one thing forever in view - the truth; and if you do this, though it may seem to lead you away from the opinion of men, it will assuredly conduct you to the throne of God".*

To go up in life and ministry, you must learn to do well! Waldo Emerson noted that: *"The stake of your life is nothing more than a reflection of the state of your mind"*. When nothing good seems to come your way, pause for a while to know whether you are good enough at doing good things. Do not judge each day by the harvest you reap, but by the seed you plant.

Never forget that if you have a demoted character before God, you will lack promotion before men! No pleasure is comparable to standing upon voltage ground of integrity. Isaac Baron did write that:

"A straight line is the shortest in morals as well as in geometry".

The unseen and unappreciated little honesty you plant in your home, office or community will be rewarded by the God of sowing and reaping!

CHAPTER 5

CREATING YOUR WORLD BY WORD

You do not have to be a talkative before you can move mountains or silence the enemy! It was just four words that separated darkness from the light. (Gen 1:3).

And God said, **Let there be light:** *and there was light.*

It was a prayer of just two sentences that brought fire from heaven. (1 Kings 18:36 -37).

> ***And it came to pass at the time of the offering of the evening sacrifice, that Elijah the prophet came near, and said, LORD God of Abraham, Isaac, and of Israel, let it be known this day that thou art God in Israel, and that I am thy servant, and that I have done all these things at thy word.***
>
> ***Hear me, O LORD, hear me, that this people may know that thou art the LORD God, and that thou hast turned their heart back again.***

It was one word, *"come"* that caused Peter to defy the laws of nature (Matt 14:29). Determine that for the rest of your life you will create and rule your world with your word. Be swift to hear, but slow to speech and anger. Your few words will suspend the laws of nature and superimpose the supernatural in your life and ministry. Remember that Michelangelo did wonders with just three colours. Remember that there are seven musical notes and yet Don Moen, Don William, Fela Anikulapo, Roney Kenoly,

Cece Winans, Kunle Ajayi etc. did and are still doing exploits with these seven notes of music!

Things can be beautiful without being complicated. Eloquence is simplicity in motion! The Queen of England made just few pronouncements in 1960 and the (Giant of Africa) Nigeria became independent!

Kings do not need plurality of words to exercise authority.

Determine to speak simply, directly and be yourself! Refuse to impress anyone with you speak the truth, be brunt and avoid high-sounding words if you can! Avoid pride! Do not let your tongue drown you. Steve Franklin; a Professor from Emory University in the US used to counsel his students:

> *"Don't ever believe that the message has to be complicated to be effective. Words do not need all four syllables to make a meaning".*

Determine to be simple and positive on daily basis for the rest of your years on earth.

Until you possess your tongue your destiny is unrealistic. Many who would have been great today are nonentities not because of anything but because of their tongue.

Many of the Israelites died in the wilderness not because God was not capable of taking them to the Promised Land, but rather because of their tongues. They confessed with their mouths that they cannot possess the land, their tongue was against their destiny, they were full of negative confession and they had to pay with their lives. Numbers 13:31 report this:

> *But the men that went up with him said, we be not able to go up against the people; for they are stronger than we.*

What you say is what you become. Many Christians today are binding and loosing, thinking that the devil is the brain behind their problems, not knowing that their tongue is what should be bound and loosened.

Many are failures today because of the fact that what comes out of their mouths are failures words, "I don't have"! "Things are tight"! "Things are tough"! "I can't make it"! "I am confused"! "I have failed"! "I don't understand what is happening"; etc.

How can a man confess negative words and not live a negative life. Hear this, your words have creative power, whatever you say is what you become. Either it is said ignorantly or knowingly, that does not matter, what you say is what you become. Because you are created in the image of God; your word has creative power as that of God: Until you start confessing good you cannot see good.

Each morning of my everyday starts with powerful confession about my life and future, even when poverty was next to my skin, I have learnt to confess prosperity. Where I am today is by the grace of God and also by the power of positive words.

Where you are today is as a result of what you said yesterday, where you will be tomorrow is as the result of what you are saying now. 1 Peter 3:10 says:

> *For he that will love life, and see good days, let him refrain his tongue from evil, and his lips that they speak no guile:*

You must understand that your thoughts become words, which become actions! Indeed your word determines the direction of your destiny! No matter what has happened in the past, determine to aggressively change your words vocabulary! Be a person known for great positive words.

Don't forget that it is the words that created this planet. It was the word that became flesh (John 1:14). It was a word *"come"* that kept Peter afloat in the storm. It was the words that were spoken by Goliath that paralyzed Saul and the Jewish Army. (1 Sam 17:11) It was the words of the ten spies that buried millions in the wilderness (Numbers 13:31; -14:1).

You must never forget that words cursed a tree (Mark 11:14-23) Words (prayer) drew early death to Samson! (Judges 16:30). Be positive person on daily basis. Let your thoughts, words, your manner, your dressing, your conversation and everything you do speak achievement! Always carry a success atmosphere with you!

You will either be enthroned or ensnared by your words; you will either be lifted or brought down by your words. Your mouth is the most important instrument you possess; don't allow it to work against you.

The thief at the right hand of Jesus Christ was justified at the last minute through his words and the one at the left hand remained condemned through his tongue.

Watch your tongue it will either justify you or condemn you. Wake up in the morning and shout at the top of your voice that *"I am a candidate of success."*

Professor Wole Soyinka, Nobel Laureate in literature commented that; *"The truth shall set you free, may be! But first, the truth must be set free".* Shakespeare also proclaimed that: ***"Men of few words are the best men"*** the truth you must discover and set free is that life and death are in the power of the tongue. (Proverbs 18:21) You must untie the hidden truth that your words determine and create your world. God created this world by what He said (Heb. 11:3). As a child of God created in His image, you can also change that mountain by your own words.

Your tongue is the pathfinder of your life, it will either limit you or leave you limitless. Until you have mastered your tongue, your destiny is unrealistic. You cannot confess evil and have good, you cannot say things are tough and not be tough.

Make this moment the right time to change the way you talk your spouse, children, Pastor, Church, your friends, your career etc. Stop complaining! Stop comparing! You eventually will get what you say! Mark 11:23, Jesus said:

> ***For verily I say unto you, That whosoever shall SAY unto this mountain, Be thou removed, and be thou cast into the sea; and shall not doubt in his heart, but shall believe that those things which he SAITH shall come to pass; he shall have whatsoever he SAITH.***

Why was Simon the former "occultic King" begging Peter thus: Pray ye the Lord for me, that none of these things which ye have spoken come upon me" (Acts 8:24). This is because Simon as a former occultic lord, understood the power of words. Yes, even the devil and the occultic world uses words to destroy, demote and derail the destiny of men.

Curses are carried by the words and they can operate till they are changed by higher words. Blessings are also carried by words. Words are the battle weapon of the spirit world. Your promotion, prosperity and purity are in your mouth. Benjamin Franklin said:

> *The heart of a fool is in his mouth, but the mouth of a wise man is in his heart.*

Apostle Paul declared: *I can do all things through Christ who strengthen me."* God want you to talk health, happiness and prosperity. The reason why many are down is because of their tongues. They are full of negative words, so they always have negative result. Positive words attract positive results while negative words attract negative results.

It is anti-success to wake up in the morning and say; "things are tough", "I don't understand what is happening", "I am down", "I am weak", "my business is down", "things are not moving well" etc.

Proverbs 18:20-21 Affirmed that:

> *A man's belly shall be satisfied with the fruit of his mouth; and with the increase of his lips shall he be filled.*

> *Death and life are in the power of the tongue: and they that love it shall eat the fruit thereof.*

Your tongue has a destiny controlling power. It will ultimately place you where you belong. Any word that comes out of your mouth is a seed planted, whether you like it or not you will reap the fruit.

Many destinies have been tied down by negative words, do not join these set of people, you have a great destiny; do not tie it down by your words. Your words mould your world, you create your world through your word. No-matter, how your situation might be, you can turn it around through your words. You can mould your destiny through your words.

Don't join men of negative word in order not to end up in negative destination. You are on course, you must win the prize.

Constantly read positive books. Speak great things and regularly dwell on positive thoughts! Avoid negative letters, newspapers or people etc that create bad feelings in you or remind you of your past! Be proud of yourself! Congratulate yourself daily, reject self-pity and depression! Choose your words daily!

CHAPTER 6

YOUR COMPANY DETERMINES YOUR DESTINATION

Life is an echo, what you send out is what you get back. People who need people are the luckiest people in the world. We all need some close supportive friend(s). Even Jesus never ministered alone, even at death and at the cross. He was crucified with people! Make time out to develop and maintain close relationships. In the day of trouble you will need them! You will also need them in your good days.

Be a good friend and purposely go out daily to make friends. One relationship can lift your destiny forever. A poet wrote: "I went out to find a friend but could not find one". I went out to be a friend and friends were everywhere. People don't care how much you know until they know how much you care - about them. George Shine wrote: *There is no such thing as a self-made man. You will reach your goals only with the help of others*". Successful people use their strength by recognizing the talents of others. The best thing about giving ourselves is that *what we get is always better than what we give*. The reaction is always greater than the action! Albert Husband:

"Best formula for having friends: Be one".

It is pathetic to note today that many has forfeited their great destines to wrong relationship.

Many who would have been great leaders today are still followers because of wrong relationship. In Proverbs 13:20; the word says:

He that walketh with wise men shall be wise: but a companion of fools shall be destroyed.

Unwise friendships and associations have stagnated the potential of millions of people who would have been famous winners today.

Many names give themselves to wrong relationships and they have ended up in wrong destinations. You must be very conscious of your relationship, choose your friends carefully. Many wanted to be close to me but I have to give them a gap because they will rob me of my destiny. Watch very well and allow the Holy Spirit to lead you to any relationship you are entering into. I love all but I have few covenant friends. Re-evaluate your life and friendship; don't allow your dreams and goals to be eroded by wrong association.

You are on a journey, you must finish the course, you are going somewhere don't allow people who are not going anywhere to stampede your vision.

Wrong association brings you to wrong destination while the right association brings you to right destination, mind your relationships. If a wise man has a foolish friend he will soon become a fool. When you spend time with a loser, you hear a loser talk; you will soon start behaving like one.

Right Relationship

¾ Those who speak words that build up confidence and faith.
¾ Those who get excited about your potential.
¾ Those who remind you of your abilities, special gifts and God's given vision.
¾ Those who are full of words of encouragement.
¾ Those who believe in your God given vision.
¾ Those who help others to increase their self-esteem, they invest in your life.
¾ Those who make you trustworthy by trusting you.

Wrong Relationship

¾Those who speak words of discouragement.

¾Those who despise your potential.

¾Those who are more critical than they are encouraging and complimentary.

¾Those who get you engaged in useless talk.

¾Those who don't believe in your God given vision.

¾Those who make you feel bad about yourself; they take away valuables from you.

¾Those who do not trust you neither your abilities.

Many who would have been masters today are still servants, wrong relationships have checked them out of their destiny. You have a bright future ahead of you; you cannot afford to lose it to wrong association. The joy of living is in fulfilment. Until you are in right company you cannot experience fulfilment. You carry the seed of greatness inside of you; don't allow wrong association to suffocate it.

The company you keep will ultimately determine your destiny. One of the things that form the life and habits of a man is the company he keeps. Show me your friend the adage says, and I will tell you who you are. The relationship you keep matters a lot to your destiny.

The relationship you keep will either increase you or decrease you, it will either add or subtract from you. It will either make your life better or make your life bitter, it will either get you to your destiny or get you farther from your destiny. Man is a product of influences, what influences you is what you ultimately become. Moving with a wrong set of people takes you to a wrong destination, while moving with a right set of people takes you to a right destination.

Everyone is a product of influences, what influences you is what you will ultimately become.

Any relationship that is not moving you forward will eventually move you backward, any relationship that is not lifting you will ultimately bring you down.

One's relationship is by choice not by force, it is advisable for you to only move with men that matter to your destiny. Walk with men that can inspire you towards fulfilling your destiny. Walk with men that can inspire you towards fulfilling your goals, not men that can draw you back. Do not stay among friends that are lazy, they will kill the zeal of hard-work in you, do not stay among the men that are busy carousing in Club Houses and going with women of easy virtue, they are dangerous to your destiny, do not talk with talkatives and busybodies. They are destiny destroyers!

Anyone that cannot inspire, challenge and motivate you towards fulfilling your life goal is injurious to your destiny. Stop him from being your friend, before he stops you from getting to your destiny. Your greatness is a function of right relationship. You need to be selective in your relationship. He who is not selective cannot be productive. Love everyone but never get committed to everyone. Your destiny is so bright but you need right companion to end up in the right destination. The world is full of people who are not going anywhere if you go with such people you automatically end nowhere.

Where you are going is so great it's not everyone that can go with you. Locate people that matter to your destiny and go with them. There is nothing as catastrophic as being in the company of people who are not going anywhere. Until you are rightly connected you cannot enjoy the right lifting.

Everyone cannot be close to you or else your destiny gets closed up. Everyone cannot be your father or else you lose your real father. Everyone cannot be your mother or else they murder your destiny.

Everyone cannot be your father or your son or else they sink you. If you are not selective you cannot be productive.

I love everyone but I don't get committed to everyone. I watch before I get committed, that has been the secret of my on-going and progressive lifting.

Friendship is by choice not by force, you have the right to select and choose those you want to be walking with; do not be too rigid to continue with a friend that has nothing to offer you. You are running a race and you must win the crown, you are meant to be a player, you cannot afford to be walking with a spectator. In a football field, players are always in the pitch playing, while spectators are busy watching and shouting to cheer up the players; after the match, the players will receive the prize while the spectators will go home empty handed because they were on the field watching others fulfil their destiny. You are meant to be a player, you don't have any reason to be a spectator, there is a prize that is awaiting you, you cannot afford to lose it by walking with the spectators. It is time to take charge; it's time for you to really become what you were created to be. You have been loaded with heavenly grace to reign, but your reigning level is a function of right relationship.

You might need to change your relationship today, because as long as you are walking with wrong people, you cannot have a right result, be bold and frank enough to part with a friend who is drawing you back, stay away from seemingly good friends who have nothing to offer you but discouragement, refuse to walk with people who are stagnant, they will make you stagnant too.

Your lifting can never outgrow your relationship; the type of people you move with will ultimately determine where you get to in life. Ask yourself these questions: Is my friend a source of inspiration and encouragement to me? Does he have something that matters to my destiny? Is he really increasing me? If not, cut him off, get new friends, decide only to move with people who are moving, not stagnant men. The success of your life is highly determined by the company you keep, Keep the right company in order to get the right result and ultimately get to the right destination. The blessing of Abraham came when Lot departed from him. Genesis 13:14–17 gives an account of this:

> *And the LORD said unto Abram, after that Lot was separated from him, Lift up now thine eyes, and look from the place where thou art northward, and southward, and eastward, and west- ward:*
>
> *For all the land which thou seest, to thee will I give it, and to thy seed forever.*
>
> *And I will make thy seed as the dust of the earth: so that if a man can number the dust of the earth, then shall thy seed also be num- bered.*

Arise, walk through the land in the length of it and in the breadth of it; for I will give it unto thee.

There are people that must depart from your life to enter your destiny. As painful as it is, letting go of the people that are not adding value to your life will be the wisest course of action. All the coercion and the coaxing in the world will not change a floundering relationship unless you work on it.

To make life work the way God intended it to, we must learn to love others, take delight in honouring others. Each of us is important, none of us is whole, independent, super-capable, all- powerful-hot-shot, let us quit acting like we are. Chose your friends carefully and meticulously! Life is hard enough without playing that silly game.

CHAPTER 7

ADDENDUM OF POSSIBILITY

Those who have reasons for failing never stop failing. Until you stop justifying impossibility your success is but a shadow.

Many people are failures today not because they are created to be, but rather because they have so called "good reasons" for settling for impossibility.

A man walked into his office one day and told his engineers. "Give me a V8 engine". He was intelligent enough to know that there had to be a V8 engine, but was ignorant and did not know how to build one. All he had was an idea. This man did not have a formal education. In fact, he did not go to school beyond the age of 14. According to his team of engineers, a V8 engine was an impossibility! Though they commended his idea, drew diagrams and sketches of what could be done, they insisted that a V8 engine was an impossible venture with all kinds of reasons. ***This man refused to give up!*** He knew that what the mind can conceive, the man can achieve. He knew that the word *"failure"* or '*impossibility*' is only found in the dictionary.of the fools. He knew that where there is a will, there must be way! He knew that delay is not denial! He knew that you can turn a disappointment into an appointment with your destiny!

So after so many months, he demanded from the engineers again: "I want my V8". Do you know that the V8 engine, which is the backbone of today's motor-cars, was produced shortly after that by the same people who said it could not be done? That dogged visionary is Mr. Henry Ford, a man who knew where he was going and defied all obstacles to get there, thereby re-writing human history! God wants you to stubbornly hold on to your life goals despite the demonic discouraging daily situations and circumstances.

Here is what James Conant said, *"Behold the Turtle; it makes progress only when it sticks out its neck"*. Joshua 14:10–12 says:

> **And now, behold, the LORD hath kept me alive, as he said, these forty and five years, even since the LORD spake this word unto Moses, while the children of Israel wandered in the wilderness: and now, lo, I am this day fourscore and five years old.** *Addendum of Possibility*
>
> **As yet I am as strong this day as I was in the day that Moses sent me: as my strength was then, even so is my strength now, for war, both to go out, and to come in.**
>
> **Now therefore give me this mountain, whereof the LORD spake in that day; for thou heardest in that day how the Anakims were there, and that the cities were great and fenced: if so be the LORD will be with me, then I shall be able to drive them out, as the LORD said.**

Caleb refused despite all the negative people and problems around him, for forty years to stop seeing where he was going! He was asking for the Mountain (a difficult terrain) when majority were looking for the valleys! Trust in the Living God and He will cause your history to change. If you stick your neck out for your course, failure will vanish, impossibility becomes possible. Don't wait for opportunity to come, go and create opportunity. Don't wait for breakthrough go and create breakthrough.

Don't sit down and be waiting for a day when someone will knock on your door and hand over a cheque of a million of your desired currency to you, it may never come.

Greatness is created not stumbled into. Have confidence in yourself. You can achieve a lot. You are better than you think.

Violate the norm. Create a throne for yourself and map out strategies to enter into the throne. Determine what you want to achieve and dedicate yourself to its attainment. Plan your progress with unswerving singleness of purpose.

Are you aware that the Taiwanese are already contemplating burning their dead on the moon? Impossible you may say! But the Houston based Celestic Inc has finalised plan for solving Taiwan's problem of serious lack of land space for new cemeteries. The firm signed a deal recently with one of Taiwan's largest Funeral Homes – Baushan Enterprise, to offer, "Space burials" to the Taiwanese! The plan is to cremate the bodies and bury the ashes on the surface of the moon! The chief executive of Celestic explained that the ashes will be packed in aluminium tube and shot into space on commercial rockets from bases in the U.S.A. and Russia. The tube orbits the earth every 90 minutes before returning to the planet and burning up! Space burials cost about 400,000 Taiwan dollars (U.S. $12,000).

Napoleon said: "The word, impossible is only found in the dictionary of fools". Determine to ignore those who say that things*Johnson. F. Odesola* can't be done! Always aim high and aim positively. "To achieve all that is possible, you must attempt the impossible." The Shunamite woman was too loaded to fail; hear what she said, "It is well. It shall be well" What are the grammars in your dictionary?

Can you ever imagine that men will be burying the dead on the moon someday? May your life break the record of impossibilities in Jesus' Name? Do you know that after Roger Bannister ran the first sub-four–minute mile, thirty seven others followed just within one year and three hundred within two years! Focus on your vision, pray prayers that defy your brain. With God all things are possible. Ronald Osborn has this to say: "*Undertake something that is difficult, it will do you good; unless you try to do something beyond what you already mastered, you will never grow*". Don't undertake any plan unless it is nearly impossible. Make possibility a key word in your life. Have you ever considered the series of inventions: The motor car, electricity or the air plane? Men and women scoffed at the ideas of these inventors!

Do you know that the best jobs have not been found? The best churches/ministries have not been crowned; the best businesses have not been registered; the best houses have not been built; the best marriages have not been sealed yet; yours can be;

the best books have not been written; the best songs have not been sung; the best sermons have not been preached; the best testimonies have not been given; believe that your rising will defy human explanation.

You may be whatever you resolve to be. Focus to be something in the world and you will become something. "I cannot" never accomplish anything. "I will try" has wrought many wonders. Re-write your vocabulary and grammar! Never be found with the word impossible. Refuse to be a fool! Nothing is impossible. Keep your hope alive.

Antonio Porchin said, *"In a full heart, there is room for everything and in an empty heart, there is no room for nothing".* Ben Fieldman advises his peers. **"Most men exchange their lifetime for much too little: Don't be afraid to think big".** Believe that you can do the most remarkable things no matter what happens. Believe that you can still wait for God concerning that miracle! People can do the incredible and unbelievable things despite the most impossible or disastrous circumstances. Do you know you can be more than you*Addendum of Possibility* are?

All humans can turn nothing into something, pennies into fortune and disaster into dancing and the reason they can do such remarkable things is because they are remarkable! There are remarkable gifts and talent in you! Paul said, you can do all things. You can change anything for yourself that you wish to change! If you don't like how something is going for you, change it! If something does not suit you; change it (except your spouse!) If something does not please you, change it! You don't ever have to be the same after reading this book! In fact, if you don't like your present haircut, or your present address, change them! *Lewis Brandles* declared that: **"Most of the things worth doing in the world had been declared impossible before they were done".** *David Thorean* says: **Public opinion is a weak tyrant; compare with our private opinion** – What a man thinks of himself that is what determines or rather indicates his fate". Believe God for the unbelievable in your life. Accept no limitations! With God you are able!

The wise doesn't expect to find life worth living; they make it that way! Jabez knew exactly the above facts! With his unfavourable circumstance of birth, he still rose as a dreamer and prospered in his generation. Hadassah

(Esther) was a "slave girl" who became a celebrity despite her being an orphan! Being focused, brave, loving God and picking determination are vital keys in making your life worth living and your biography a best seller! Read from Osho Indian: *"You will find meaning in life only if you create it. It is not there like a rock that you will find. It is a poetry to be composed; it is a song to be sung; it is dance to be danced"*

Obstacles don't have to stop you. If you run into a brick wall, don't turn around and give up. Figure out how to climb it, but never quit! Life is like a blank cheque given to you by God! Be careful what you fill in and claim from life. *The wise don't wait for things to happen; they make them happen within the limits of God's will.* Do you know that despite the daily blood bath, nightmare and dealings on the streets of troubled areas of the world people are still getting married, building houses and moving their life forward? Your life is in your hands. All things are possible to you if you believe (Mark 9:23). It is possible to make your life worthwhile.

CHAPTER 8

STOP JUSTIFYING FAILURE

So many people will have scores of reasons about why they are not where they are supposed to be; "Suppose I was born into a rich family I would have made it. Suppose I was born into a particular country I would have made it, suppose I had a good educational background I would have made it".

I have seen many people born into a rich home yet they are less than a pauper. I have seen people born into the so-called great countries yet they are failures.

Have you heard about John Foppe, a 34 years old man born without arms and with seven other birth "mistakes" that confirms this. To several on the earth today, that would have been a good reason to blame God daily for their conditions and develop self-pity, comparison and self-blame. But for Mr. Foppe, he cooks, eats, drinks, drives and operates his computer with his legs. A Master degree holder and the author of an inspirational and personal growth book called: *What's your Excuse? Making the Most of what you have*". No matter your setbacks, obstacles or barriers, your life is a product beyond excuses.

Obstacles are up-starters; set-backs are stepping stones! Though Moses was a stammerer, he shook his generation! Though David seems to be the last-born, he excelled! Though Elijah had no money, the God of miracles met his needs through a raven. Though Jeremiah was inexperienced, unconnected, uneducated and little, the God of promotion made him a power broker in his generation. Don't forget that Plato was a hunchback! M K O Abiola started from poverty level! Thomas Edison was poor! Roosevelt was paralysed from the waist! Beethoven was deaf! Abraham Lincoln had serious setbacks! Martin Luther Jnr was black! What is that excuse Satan is showing you! Shun it and wage war against it!

Your lifting is not determined by your location, but rather by your connection, not by your background but rather your backbone. Once God is your Father you are super-connected. It is not your altitude that determines your attitude but rather your attitude determines your altitude. When you are connected to God you are through.

People are not moved by excuses but rather by results, people are not moved by complaints but rather by achievement. No one wants to know how many stumbling blocks are before you, people want to know how you have been able to turn those stumbling blocks into stepping stones on your way to the top to the top.

The way to win applause from the world is not by complaining but rather by winning. There are many complainers but there are few winners. The world is interested in winners not complainers. Stop complaining, stop justifying failure, go ahead and win; turn your test to testimony, turn your trial into triumph, crush those failure stones and make a success block out of it. Don't sit down and start telling people reasons why you are not making it, tell the people how you have been able to make headway, despite contradictory situations and circumstances. Don't prove to be a victim of circumstances. Don't turn yourself into an object of pity by telling people the stories of failure, but rather make yourself a dignified personality by telling people how you have made it in spite of all odds.

The world is looking for *"encouragers"* not *"discouragers"*. Once you are an "encourager" you have automatically won a throne for yourself, then you are on your way to become a celebrity. Success has its own reward; you can't afford not to experience it. Your achievement is what takes you to the Hall of fame and celebrity, not your complaints.

It is amazing that Michael Jordan, one of the greatest success stories of basketball worldwide said, ***"I have failed over and over and over again in my life and that is why I am a success today"***. He equally told the group of young-stars! "If you're trying to achieve, there must be road blocks. I've had them: everybody has had them. But obstacles do not have to stop you! If you run into a wall, do not turn around and give up. Figure out how to climb it, go through it, or walk around it." God is saying to someone that no matter the faults and defects in your life there is a success locked up within you. Don't despair! Did something good not come out of Nazareth, a despised city?

Allow God to use you to show others the good in them. Help others to realize they can overcome their faults. What was the secret behind the wonderful success of Joseph? God believes in you just as Joseph's father believed in him (Gen 37:3) and made him a coat of many colours! Yes, there are potentials (coats of many colours) in every soul. The first thing his brethren did to Joseph was to strip. him of his coat of many colours (Gen. 37:23).

> *And it came to pass, when Joseph was come unto his brethren, that they stript Joseph out of his coat, his coat of many colours that was on him;*

That's Satan plan – to blind your eyes to the good in you and make you feel you are nobody, dull and with a colourless future. No! Resist him! Despite your past or present failure. Don't allow any devil to take away your coat of many colours. It is tears that produce triumph! Rejection provokes selection! Crying produces cruising! Your misery is what your ministry becomes".

It was Alvin Day who wrote: *"sometime you must fight and win, just because all the pain and suffering you experienced up to that point on your quest would be rendered futile if you were to surrender now".*

It is too late to give up!

Whatever field you might be, go ahead and become a celebrity, go ahead and become an achiever, go ahead and become a winner, don't yield to circumstances, let circumstances yield to you, don't yield to situations, let situation bow at your feet, don't allow problems to bow you down, bow down problems. Don't allow breakdown, give in to breakthrough, you are running a race, you must win the crown.

You don't become a failure by others' recommendation but rather by your acceptance. If Jabez has justified failure, he would have died a failure (1 Chronicles 4:9–10). Instead for Jabez to sit down and begin to blame God for creating him a failure, he rather stood up, he cried to God with strong determination and dedication and God changed his destiny. There is a great future ahead of you but it can only become a reality when you refuse to justify failure, because people are failing in your environment does not give you an excuse for failing, you can decide to stand out among the crowd. No justifiable reason to fail, failure is an abuse of your personality.

The question for each man to settle is not what he would do if he has the means, time, influence and educational advantages, but what he would do with the things he has. Forget about lamenting about what/where you should have been! God can take you to where you ought to be if you shun making excuses for failure.

Your concern should not be what you have lost, but what you have left. Stop looking back, like Elisha asked the woman **"What hast thou in the house?"** (2 Kings 4:2). God asked Moses in Exodus 4:2; **"What is that in thine hand?"** It's true that Moses had lost his power, prestige and position for 40 years, but there was something he still had! *"No matter how your past has been or how much you have lost, you have not and can never lose everything. There is always something left for God to use".*

Note that opportunity is always where you are, never where you were! Teddy Roosevelt counselled: **"Do what you must do with what you have, where you are".** Ken Keys Junior said: **"To be upset over what you don't have is to waste what you do have".** Epicurus has this to say: **"Do not spoil what you have by desiring what you have not: but remember that you can never arrive until you begin where you are".** So stop the regrets, depression, self-comparison and you excuse lamentation for failure.

All is not lost! A zero can become a hero! Hold on to hope! All great people were given strong evidence, (reasons) why they could not be great! Consider the following: Albert Einstein was four years old before he could read anything. He was advised by his teachers to drop out of School. But today how many scientists are greater than him? Few! One great Nigeria lawyer, Senior Advocate and publisher of repute, Gani Fawehinmi made Third Class in Law at the University. But today there are few Lawyers in Nigeria that have achieved more than him! The Revered Literature Nobel prizewinner, Professor Wole Soyinka also made a Third Class at the University. Assuming Albert Einstein, Gani and Soyinka dwelt on self-pity, self-comparison and excuse, would they be stars today?

Don't forget that failure doesn't mean you are a failure! It just means you have not succeeded yet! Truly life is a grinding stone. Whether it grinds you down or polishes you up depends on what you are made of! Vince Lombardi wrote: ***It is not whether you get knocked down, it is whether you get up again that counts"***. In the "dictionary" of success of Abraham Lincoln he boldly declared to his senators: "Always bear in mind that your own resolution to succeed is more important than anyone thing". Just before David killed Goliath, he had three visible evidences from Eliab (his eldest brother), King Saul and Goliath himself, why he could not win! Such is life. Problems and people will show up daily to remind you that you cannot make it! Shout them down! Roger Babson says: ***"If things go wrong, don't go with them"***.

I once went for a preaching engagement in one of the Southern Countries in Africa and the host Bishop was telling me some so called "good reasons" on why the Church has not been growing in the area, to him he had a genuine reasons, however, to me it was a flimsy excuse, I saw him as a man who has lost his throne to failure through scores of excuses. I sat down with him in Godly dialogue and counsel to impact something into him that could make him to go ahead in spite of the situation and circumstances, today things have changed with him, the Church he is overseeing is now growing. When he stopped having excuses he stopped failing. ***Until you stop justifying failure you will never stop experiencing it.***

Red Wood Trees are the tallest living things on earth, but their heights are being limited no matter how ideal the conditions. A study of what is presently the world tallest tree (110 meters, about the height of a 30 storey building) shows that the maximum height that a Red Wood may reach is about 130 meters and not 110 meters. This limitation in height is due to the fact that as moisture evaporates from the leaves, water has to be pulled up from the roots through the tubes called "Zylem Vessel". This creates great tension, which cuts off the supply, thus limiting the tree's height. In like manner, excuses will cut off progress heights and limit your growth to success in many areas of life.

Have you not seen various encomiums in the newspaper in the obituaries' section with connotations of praise and impartation of greatness and goodness upon the dead. We read things like, ***"He was a meticulous,*** *gifted and excellent administrator of no mean order". "He was the best Governor that the State never had".* Must you die before people or generations discover your talent or your divine assignment? Discover it fast! Stop giving excuses for your failure! No mortal lives forever! No amount of praise after death can bring your greatness back! There is greatness within you! Stop justifying failure that biting problem or obstacle should not stop you! Sitting down to lament your fate will only bring you nearer to your grave. *This world does not owe you any apology.* Jimmy Durante said: *"If you want rainbow, you've got to put up with the rain.* It is true that Henry Kissinger said: *"Each success only buys an admission ticket to more problems", but never forget that no excuse maker has ever won.*

Be aware of some secret formulae in the laboratory of God; consider some: The way to the throne is through the Cross; the way to triumph is through tears! The way up is down! The manger or the pit is the genesis of the place! (Genesis 45:1-11). It is nonsense that stimulates sense! Nothing gives birth to something! Pain produces gain (Genesis 50:20). Death is the father of life! Rubbish is the rocket *Stop Justifying Failure* that fires destinies (Nehemiah 4:2). Yes, the devil did not know that crucifying Jesus (a disgraceful death) was actually God's plan for glorifying Jesus! It is disgrace that stimulates grace. It is shame that produces honour. Delay is the father of ultimate dominion, delay is not denial; stop this excuses.

CHAPTER 9

DO YOU HAVE A DESTINATION? WHERE?

Give yourself a course! Do you have a destination? Where exactly are you going?

How and where will your life story end? To begin is very important, but your ultimate destination is much more important. What Satan attacks is purpose (Ezra 4:5) because he knows it is very crucial! Where are you going? Dr. Rison Marden said: ***"The man who succeeds has a programme"***. Too many people are like the person who flung himself on his horse and rode off in all directions at the same time! David Jordan wrote: *"The world stands aside to let anyone pass that knows where he is going"*. Set yourself a destination, draw a plan for getting there and follow this up with ruthless determination to succeed.

Destination is a function of personal decision not a chance. Whatever you become in life is a direct function of your choice. Whatever destination you arrive in life is the choice that you made that landed you there. Good people can make bad choices just as bad people can make good choices. ***"The fact is that we are all a sum total of all our past choices"***. Our past was shaped by the choices we made in the past. Our future will be shaped by the choices we make today. No matter how your life must have been, you can choose where you are going. You can choose to maintain your joy and choose to continue looking to God for a bright future. You can choose to reject self-pity, self-comparison and depression. You can choose to start a new beginning for your life. Choose also to pray, remember, prayer does not change things. Prayer changes everything! Great men have something in common and that is the strong decision to make the most out of life.

Greatness is not stumbled into; it's consciously acquired through strong personal decision and focus.

You need to personally set out with strong decision to make it. Don't just expect things to change for you overnight, you need a personal decision.

Decide your destination and make up your mind to be the best of whatever you are. Douglas Malloch penned down the following: *Do you have a destination? Where?*

If you can't be a pine on top of the hill. Be a shurp in the valley but be
The best little shurp by the side of the hill. Be a bush if you can't be a tree.

If you can't be a bush be a bit of grass
And some highway happier make
If you can't be a muskie just be a bass
But be the liveliest bass in the lake.

We can't all be captains: we've got to be crew. There is something for all of us.
There is big work to do and there is lesser to do
And the task we must do is the near.

If you can't be a highway then just be a trail. If you can't be a sun be a star
It isn't by size that you win or you fail.
Be the best of whatever you are.

The secret of success is strong decision of your destination and the focus to make it there.

Decide where you are going and then reach into that destination!

Nothing can stop a man who has a destination! You can be successful; it's up to you! There is no short cut to success.

Do not wait for someone to decide your destination, know where you are going and be aware of your direction; be careful not to misplace your ticket of description of your bus–stop.

The illustration below will further drive home my point of emphasis here. On board on a train is Professor Albert Einstein. Though recognized as one of the greatest minds/inventors in science, he misplaced his ticket. During the search, which followed, the train conductor kept saying to Einstein: "Take it easy Sir, you will find it". After a while of futile search, the conductor told Einstein: "Sir, you are a popular man. This transport company knows you bought a ticket, so forget about it and enjoy your ride." Einstein replied, the conductor thus; "You are very kind, but I must find it otherwise, I won't know where to get off this train." The direction and destination were pinned to the ticket! Likewise many people proceed through life without a clear picture of where they are going.

There was this story of Mr. "Follow D" Crowd. He went to the college of his friend's choice! He pursued a history major solely because his girlfriend had also chosen that major. He took a job with certain company because his friend thought it was a good firm. Mr. Follow D C. moved to a large new home because a colleague had just purchased one. He bought a new car because his neighbour has one. One of his friends told him of a new investment, so he signed on even with borrowed money. Many months later, the company folded up and the investment collapsed!

My Follow also lost his job, his new house and his fancy car. And most painful of all, his friends who he had been following were nowhere in sight. They had disappeared! Mr. Follow realized that crowd is only there in times of prosperity. He painfully realized what Benjamin Disraeli said; *'Nothing can resist a human will that will stake even its existence on the extent of its purpose!'* Where are you going? Refuse to follow the crowd! Don't be moulded into the image of others. Let God's will and your destination in life be your reason for all you do. Edward De Bono did say: *"You don't dig a new well by digging the same hole deeper".* Get out of following people that have no destination. God hates this, you must also hate it! Great men of history are men that have given themselves to a course. *The shortest route to failure is trying to be in many roads and many fields at a time* "Jack of all trade; is master of none".

You don't become a star by jumping from one place to another or from one career to another but rather by giving yourself to a course. Jesus gave Himself to a course - dying on the cross to redeem mankind. Mungo

Park had a goal – discovering the sea route to Niger – Henry Ford had a goal – designing on automobile with four wheels. An attempt to be known everywhere and in every field will make you a failure in disguise.

There is a reason for living, discover it and give yourself to it. Until you give yourself wholly to a course you cannot become somebody, your success and your shining is attached to a course, discover that course and give yourself to it. There might be distractions, refuse to give yourself to distraction, there might be obstacles, refuse to give yourself to this, make up your mind never to be satisfied until you have finished your course.

You are empowered to succeed; you must give yourself to a course in order to become a shining star! Apostle Paul gave himself to a course, he gave himself to the course of the gospel, he left footprint on the sand of time. Here is what he said: "I have fought a good fight, I have finished my course, I have kept the faith (2 Timothy 4:7).

This man had a target, he has a destination and he made it there.

It takes a man who has given himself to a course to be able to talk like Paul. Paul gave himself to the course of the gospel and he became a shining star.

Since the day I discovered that I have been created to be a Minister of the gospel, I gave myself totally to it. Nothing enticed me like preaching the gospel, nothing excites me like seeing souls won, nothing thrills me like seeing people healed and delivered by the power of the Lord! I have discovered the essence of my living and I have given myself to it, I wake up to think of the gospel, my whole thought is on evangelism, my whole being responds spontaneously to the course of the gospel – that is the essence of my life. I have found the reason for my living.

Dear friend, what are you living for? What is the course you are supposed to run? Discover it and give yourself to it, you are not created to be a failure; you must not die a failure. Don't play with your life, you are running a race, you must win the prize.

Every star is always known for something, they are always remember in a particular field. If you remember Shakespeare you remember a great author, if you remember Charles G. Finney you remember a great revivalist, if you remember Martin Luther you remember a great revolutionist; if you remember Ayo Babalola you remember a prayer champion! Each of these men are known for something, they were authorities in their individual fields. Give yourself to a course doggedly and you can be sure of spontaneous lifting.

Being a part–time businessman, a part-time teacher and also at the same time a part-time security guard automatically makes you a part-time failure. Once a man gets involved into too many things at a time failure is inevitable.

One of the shortest routes to failure is getting involved into too many things at the same time. Inefficiency sets in when a man gets involved into too many things at a time and inefficiency is the mother of failure. It is not how many fields you are in that makes you great, it is how efficient you are in your field.

The level of the honour you enjoy from people is largely determined by the level of result you have in your chosen career and not how many fields you have been, once you can doggedly hold on to a course you can become a star on it, then you can be sure of success rewards.

Stardom and grandeur come as a result of knowing your destination and you keep on until you get there.

CHAPTER 10

STOP IMITATING THE DEFEATED

The word "impossible" is devastating in its effects on the subconscious mind. Thinking stop! Progress halts! Doors slam shut! Research comes to a screeching halt! Further experimentation is damaged! Projects are abandoned! Dreams are discarded! The brightest and the best of the creative brain cells are nose-driven, claim up, hide out, cool down and turn off in some dark but safe corner of the mind!

However, when you echo forcefully *"it might be possible!"* I don't know how, or when, but it is possible." Those stirring words with the siren appeal of a marshalling trumpet penetrates into the subconscious tributaries of the mind, changing and calling those proud powers to turn on and turn out! Buried dreams are resurrected! Sparks of fresh enthusiasm flicker, then burst into flames.

Dusty files are reopened! Telephone starts ringing again! Factories are re-tooled and reopened! New product appears! New markets open! Resist the word *"impossible"* because it is a dangerous demon. It has the destructive power of an emotional thermonuclear bomb: *'impossible"* that word is a knife at the heart of creativity! It is a roadblock to progress!

Nothing is impossible in this life! Failure is only a temporary setback! This is the mentality of the winner! Nothing is impossible to him that believeth! Know thyself!

"You can do all things through Christ who strengthens you" (Philippians 4:13). Discover yourself! You have limitless power, because the limitless God lives in you! You are unbeatable because the man of war dwells within you.

You cannot die prematurely because the hands that hold the world are enwrapped around you! You cannot be weak for the Lord is the strength of your life! Your family cannot beg for bread because the El-shaddai. (Multi breasted God) is your shepherd! Loaded creative ideas lie within you because you are an extension of the divine omniscience! Greatness is in you! Health, wisdom, riches are in you if you believe all things are possible. Nothing can frustrate you, because if God be for you, who can be against you? Nothing is impossible to you if you believe in the God with whom all things are possible! Scratch the word, *"impossible"* out of your vocabulary then watch progress, upward development and creative breakthrough emerge.

Walt Disney said: ***"It is a kind of fun to do the impossible".*** Jesus the voice of divinity had given the world a bomb shell that, ***"all things are possible to him that believe".*** Charles Schwab noted that: ***"People can succeed at almost anything for which they have unlimited enthusiasm".***

Believe God, that you will reach level considered impossible and that you will break that record of impossibility, in your family, career and life endeavors. Ponder on these: Simon Dayange sat on top of a stone in Syria for 45 years without standing up!

Mrs. Billoid Vaseline gave birth to 69 Children in 27 births. She had 16 pairs of twins, 7 sets of triplets and four sets of quadruplets.

Amras Kumol Jarbiha of India stood on one leg for 7 hours 40 minutes in 1995.

Joan Rustin an Austrian in 1990 did 18,070 miles on hands to set an endurance record in the Guinness Book of Records.

All these listed records are unbelievable and to the natural mind, it is impossible, yet they were accomplished by men – mere mortals like you! Do you know you can endure longer on any matter? You are the architect of your future and your fortune! Think big! Make no small plans! Enlarge your coat of faith and shame will never locate your address forever.

Wilma Baker in the book 'A Savior for all seasons' relates the story of a bishop from the east coast, who many years ago, paid a visit to a small Midwestern religious college. He stayed at the home of the college president, who also served as a professor of physics and chemistry. After dinner the bishop declared that the millennium could not be far off because just about everything about nature has been discovered.

The young college President politely disagreed and said he felt there would be many more discoveries and inventions. When the angry Bishop challenged the President to name first one of such invention, the president replied that he was certain that within 50 years, men would be able to fly.

"Non-sense! Only Angels are intended to fly", shouted the visibly angry bishop. The Bishop's name was Wright and he had two boys at home who would prove to have greater vision, insight and extra determination to conquer than their father. Their names are Orville and Wilbur and they both invented the aero plane! Think about that! When things look difficult and impossible or when they defy your brain and imagination, you must continue to hold on, because it is possible. Samuel Johnson wrote that: *"Nothing will ever be attempted if all possible objections must first be overcome".* The impossible will bow when you hold on. With God all things are possible (Luke 1:37). Charles Swindol said: *"Nothing is so common as unsuccessful men with talents. They only lack determination".* Don't be in that group. William Feather also said; *"success seems to be largely a matter of hanging on after others have let go".* Hang On!

When the world said it was *impossible*; Chester Carlson discovered Xerography (a photocopying process that uses dry powder exposed to electricity and light!). When the world concluded it was not possible Edwin Land produced the Polaroid Camera and Film. Don't forget the story of the Wright Brothers, who saw what their father could not see!

It was Rodent Fulton who discovered the steamship in the midst of severe criticisms! What about the scientific giant Isaac Newton who was written off as "too dull to remain in class" Has it ever occurred to you that, *"those who dance are thought mad by those who do not hear music"*! Jairus was told concerning his daughter, it was over – (Luke 8:49). The woman with the issue of blood went through a crowd of opposition, but in-spite of this, she laughed at the end. No matter how old you are and no matter how long you have waited and prayed, your laughter will soon manifest.

You must hold on with all within you! Napoleon said: *"Victory belongs to the most persistent"* Montesquiell also did announce: *"Success in most things depends on knowing how long it takes to succeed".*

Louis Armstrong told his determined colleagues: *"Pain is temporary. It may last a minute, or even an hour or even a day or even a year, but eventually, it will subside and something else will take its place. If I quit, however, it last forever".*

There is no great name in life that has not passed through *"Mistake Avenue* & *Failure Crescent"*. They are compulsory addresses for every destined winners. Stop crying! Forgive yourself and stop imitating the fool's vocabulary. Michael Jordan says: *"I can accept failure, everyone fails at something. But I can't accept not trying"*. Unless you are willing to have a go, to fail miserably and have another go, success won't happen.

Never use the word, *"impossible"* seriously again toss it into the waste basket. Hear Thomas Edison: "I will burn all bridges behind me and stake my entire future on my ability to get what I want. It is true that hope lives in the future, but dies in the present, but never forget that hope tackles impossibilities.

Charles Dickens affirmed: Ride on, Rough Shod if need be, smooth Shod if that will do, but ride on! Ride on over all obstacles and win the race.

Most men exchange their lifetime for much too little. Don't be afraid to move on to dare impossibility.

Between you and anything of worth in life, there are giants. However, you must fight anything that will limit your life and coast! If your relationship will limit you change them! If your job limits you, change it! If your Church limits you, change it. If your name limits you, Change it. If your accommodation limits you, change it! If the bed you sleep on limits you from your Spiritual night exercise, sleep on something else! If you're TV or computer or anything in your home limits you, sell them!

See to it that you fight against the agents of impossibility and limitation. Nothing changes if nothing changes! God is set to do more for you and through you in the remaining days of your stay on this earth. How would you feel if you had no fear? Feel like that. How would you behave to other people if you realize their powerlessness to hurt you? Behave like that! How would your reaction to so called misfortunes be if you saw a weight of goodness and fortune contained therein? React like that! How would you think toward yourself if you knew you were all right and not inferior to anybody? Think like that! Stop imitating the fools! Your mind is the breeding ground of success!

Obstacles can't stop you! Problems can't stop you. Most of all, other people can't stop you! Only you can stop yourself. (Jeffrey Gitomer). The difference between an obstacle and an opportunity is our attitude towards them. The travel is worth of the travail when you are on the right track. You are on the right track of possibility.

CHAPTER 11

INVEST YOUR PAINS INSTEAD OF WASTING IT

Life's disappointments are opportunities hidden appointments. A Christian Sister called Alice had a mysterious abdominal pain that made her to question the love, faithfulness and the integrity of God! For months, she visited Doctors who did the tests but never found the problems! Finally a new Doctor referred her to a local gastroenterologist (a special Doctor on the stomach).The gastroenterologist did a tests and discovered diverticulosis (The cause of the sharp pains). The tests further revealed that lots of polyps (a growth/tumour which can progress to cancer) were in the body. The Doctor removed one of the polyps only to discover after the test that the polyps were pre-cancerous. A following visit to the gastroenterologist confirmed that if polyps were not discovered due to the sharp pain she experienced, it was possible that they would have grown into full-grown colon cancer in about a year from then!

Truly, God works in a mysterious ways, His wonders to perform! Whatever circumstance or event you do not fully understand and cannot explain: please always give thanks! It would make your testimony more famous! The mystery of salvation is that it was hidden in the ages from angelic understanding. This was why the angels could not understand why Jesus had to die (Peter 1:12).

Lots of times, there are lots of gain that can only be experienced through pain. The Almighty God will never allow any circumstance that will cause pain to produce further pain. It must end up in gain! Truly every obstacle introduces a person to himself! Give thanks to God even in pain and crisis! It would promote you! No wonder in *"As you like it,"* Shakespeare wrote:

"Sweet are the use of adversity, which like a toad, ugly and venomous, find tongues in trees, books, in the running brooks, sermons in stones and good in everything". Hold on to God, good is coming out of that pain. Nothing just happens in your life! God will only permit and engineer the event and circumstances that will end up lifting you. A record had it that in 1932 one of the African evangelists and founders of Christ Apostolic Church, Joseph Ayo Babalola was unjustly imprisoned for 6 months for an offence he never committed by the then colonial government. The two diabolical women in Otuo (presently in Edo State Nigeria), falsely accused him of forcing them to drink a poisonous local herb used in detecting witchcraft possession and which the government had banned! Despite the strong denial by the great prophet with collaborating witnesses that he had never met any of the two women, he was sent to prison in the ancient city of Benn for six months. Indeed according to Roman 8:28; which says all things work together for good to those who love God. So, while in prison, the God that can turn a thorn into a throne began to manifest. In prison he met a Greek man (from Greek town in Calabar, Nigeria) named Cyprian Ufon who was healed instantly after Babalola prayed for him! After the release from prison, their divinely planned meeting eventually led to the explosion of the missionary work to the eastern part of Nigeria!

Is it not a mystery to the carnal man that God sent Moses, His choice servant to "Professor" Jethro as a student for forty years in the "University of Wilderness" based in Median?

Surely it is beyond our explanation that the "prime minister in waiting" Joseph should pass through the pit and the prison to the palace!

Why must Paul and Silas get into prison unjustly in order to enable the gospel into Macedonia? (Europe) through the jailer!

You need to know that the strength of a man consists in finding out the way God is going and follow the going. Every pathway of pain allowed into your life is for a specific reason, which you will discover later.

Roosevelt ruled as a President of the U.S.A. from a wheelchair. Let the Lord turn your story into glory! Never cry! Paul's thorn enabled him to bless his generation! Invest your pain.

The greatest motivator of her time was Helen Keller. She was deaf and blind! Allow God to turn any setback or adversity for your good. The allowed pain is a "Prophet" that will announce your life and lifting. Thorns can become thrones, scars can become stars, vices can become visions, your frustration can become your expressions, if you will allow God to finish His chemical reaction in your life's laboratory. In the shell of an Oyster (an invertebrate like a snail), a tiny grain of sand finds its way. The intruder (the grain of sand) though microscopic, is a source of irritation and pain to the soft body of the Oyster. Unable to rid itself of the unwelcome grain of sand, the Oyster seeks to adjust and reduce the pain by coating the sand grain with layers of soft materials from its own shell. Over the time, the Oyster transforms a pain and irritating condition (grain of sand) into a beautiful heap of stones of great value, which are called pearls. A pearl is a gem or precious stone, which is of very high value as gold or diamond. But do you know that pearls are produced from the pains of an Oyster? The truth is that most of us have unwelcome "grains of sand" or annoying situation that comes our ways as we journey through life. No wonder then when Anne Baxter said: ***"Something good always comes out of failure"***. Shakespeare also wrote, "Sweet are the uses of adversity." Years ago green Ingersoll said: ***"Happiness is not a reward, it is a consequence."*** So determine to turn every difficulty into something wonderful. I Thessalonians 5:18 Says: *"....in all things give thanks for this is the will of God for you in Christ Jesus"*.

One of the African proverbs says: ***"The bigger a man's head, the worse his headache"***. Your trials are sometimes much because your star is very bright. Consider the suffering of the Jews as a nation! Consider the Holocaust in which six million of them died! Consider the gas chambers of Auschwitz. It is not because there is no nation on the earth today with the type of destiny of Israel. Determine to wait till that test becomes a testimony. Refuse to complain or explain. Wait for God to turn that pain into a pearl.

Don't see yourself as living with a problem. See yourself as living with a challenge! Don't forget that everyone has one problem or the other! But like Darcy E. Cubbons said: ***"Success is just a matter of attitude."*** Attitude is your pattern of thinking! Mercus Antonuis said: ***Our life is what our thoughts make it"***. Proverbs 23:7; Says, "As he (a man) thinketh, so is he......" Henry D. Thoreau noted that: ***"What a man thinks of himself determines or rather indicates his fate"***. So, no matter what you are going through, always remember that you will eventually become what you think! See every problem as a challenge and with the grace of God, you will overcome. Be positive about life. Laugh at the devil. Remind him that because Jesus lives you can face tomorrow. Refuse to complain. A set back is a set up for a comeback. Job said in Job 19:25 that

> ***"For I know that my redeemer liveth, and that he shall stand at the latter day upon the earth:"***

Always remind yourself to declare, ***"I know I will make it ..."*** No matter how long it takes, I know my testimony shall shine forth. Men shall cerebrate with me because my pain is the genesis of gain.

It is important to understand that life is a School. Everyday is designed for learning. If a man refuses to learn a lesson from his daily experience he may not graduate in life.

Whatever you pass through in life is meant to teach you a lesson, if you refuse to learn a lesson from your daily experience you may not arrive in your God- designed destination.

Life is full of instructors and teachers, everyone you meet in life teaches you one lesson or the other, some teach you good lessons, while others teach you bad lessons.

Your daily encounter is designed to nurture you and make out you what you are really designed to be. Your daily experience is not meant to break you but to make you; it is not designed for your down fall but rather for your uplifting. Always see life from a positive angle because the way you see your life is what it will turn out to be.

Ask yourself, what God is communicating to you from your present situation. At times you might pass through crisis in order to build up your inner stamina. God may allow people to leave your life in order for you to build your trust in God. Every pain you pass through will end up in giving you more power. There is power in pain. There is lifting in downfall. There is blessing in hardship.

Don't allow any situation to come and pass without a lesson from it. Maturity is not a function of age but ability to combine the past experiences and make it to work for you. What you are passing through is not as important as what you gain from it.

A wise man once wrote to his sister who was complaining and murmuring about how unfair life has been to her: ***"life is a grinding*** *stone! Whether it grinds you down, polishes you up, depend on what you are made of"*. Put to mind what Senaca said: *"The worst evil of all is to leave the ranks of the living before one dies"*. Living with regrets and refusal to accept the fact that the trials of life are the root of triumph, is like slow death. You must face the bitter realities that life is a School! Suffering is part of life and perfection comes through pain. *The bitter mystery of life is that motion is smoothened only by friction! Rest is only enjoyed after war!*

Why does the deep darkness improve the brightness of the star?

Envy no one because the load "pain" and the street called "pleasure" are compulsory routes to the top. Face life with your God and fight! No one owes you any apology. You are here alone with your God. Let God top your agenda and priorities.

Your swimming or sinking does not depend on anybody. Don't trust men! Be determined to turn every adversity into an opportunity and every failure into a stepping-stone to permanent*Invest your pains instead of wasting it* laughter. Nobel Laureate in literature, Professor Wole Soyinka was in prison when he wrote his prison notes, which were later, compiled into his famous book "The man died". Though he is a gifted writer, his traumatic experience behind the bars provoked his creative faculties. As a matter of fact, the book "The man Died" is one of his major works considered before he was awarded the Nobel Prize for literature. His untold story of success is called suffering. It is a step in the ladder of success.

The truth is that nobody desires pain or suffering, but suffering reveals your best-hidden talents or your worst hidden characters! Suffering and pain are revelations! They are allowed by God to perfect your journey through planet Earth. Hebrews 2:10;

> *"For it became him, for whom are all things, and by whom are all things, in bringing many sons unto glory, to make the captain of their salvation perfect through sufferings."*

Why did God allow Joseph to suffer innocently for a crime he did not commit? God is a great Mathematician. No allowed suffering is permanent. *When you are down to nothing; God is up to something.* Trust Him! Hold on to God even in the darkest valley or on the loneliest mountain!

Pressure is what provokes pleasure! Problems are only opportunities in work clothes. Vince Lombardi said: *"In great attempts, it is glorious even to fail."* Pain is the genesis of every notable gain. So never allow self-pity of depression into your life because pains or trials are the necessary and unavoidable bus stops to your great destiny! Forget that disappointment and move on! Mary Kay Ash Says: *"Winners must fail forward to success"* Keep looking forward! Hold on to God, for your expectation shall not and cannot be cut off, because they that wait on the Lord shall never be put to shame!

CHAPTER 12

FEAR OF THE UNKNOWN MAKES YOU UNKNOWN

Countless number of people who would have been achievers are held captives by fear. Fear has sent who would have been great today into obscurity. Fear of failure has made many who would have been great business magnates today to be servants and clerks in offices. What will happen if I fail? What will people say? The first step is never taken because of fear. Fear of the unknown has made them unknown. Can you imagine millions that have gone down to their graves without realizing their full potentials because of fear?

Nothing implicates life more than fear, nothing destroys like fear. Fear is a force that must be crushed into pieces by everyone who really means to get to the top in life.

Fear not! Try again! Take a risk again! Never resist opportunities and never rehearse impossibilities because today's impossibilities are tomorrow's possibilities. Never review your inadequacies. Face your inadequacies and look to the Almighty God! Never replace goals with pleasure because of fear! Never reject the personal cost of your goals! Never resist change if you must! Never allow procrastination or fear to keep you from any necessary step/action/project.

Mr. Sidney said: *"Regret for the things we did can be tempered by time. It is the regret for the things we did not do that is inconsolable"*. If you take risks and fail, you will have fewer regrets than if you do nothings and fail! Listen to Dick Butler as you prepare and allow God to fire your destiny into new heights. *"Life isn't fair! It isn't going to be fair! Stop wishing and whining and go out and make it happen for you".* Without faith, it is impossible to please God; fear is the opposite of faith, so determine to walk exclusively by faith. Roman 14:23b says: *"Whatsoever is not of faith is sin".* Take a step of faith (risks) and watch your borders enlarge!

Wishing that a risk wasn't yours to take won't make it easier! There is nothing so fatiguing as the external hanging on of an uncompleted task. A risk is not a foolish action! Let your mission statement be: *"I would rather try something great and fall than try nothing great and succeed".* Little progress is better than no progress at all. Determine to move on! Never let fear stop you.

Many who would have been great employers today are carrying around application letters looking for somebody to employ them. Fear checked them out of their destiny. There are many people who would have been pastoring thousands of people today but fear didn't allow them to step out and start what God wants them to do; many of these are still walking around like new converts, fear has checked them out of their destiny. Fear is one of the greatest obstacles to success, it stagnates and makes one useless. It is the route and the cornerstone of many failures; until you get rid of fear your destiny is not realistic.

Fear of failure is the route to failure; no one gets to the top without getting rid of it.

A failure is not the one that attempts something worthwhile and do not achieve it but the one for fear of failure didn't try at all.

You don't become a failure by trying; you become a failure by not attempting at all.

Fear tears destiny, bewares of it.

Is it not true that problems are opportunities in disguise? Is it not true that choice, not chance determines all human destinies? Is it not a wonder that the winner of the 100 meter race (also the fastest woman on earth) during the 1960 Olympics was paralysed at the age of four due to the disease called polio? She was Wilma Rudolph born into poor home in Tennessee, in the U.S.A. Due to the triple attack of Pneumonia, Fever and Polio, She was paralyzed and the Doctor said, "She must wear a brace through her days on the planet earth". In her bedridden state, as she heard stories of sport heroes and heroines, she said she made up her mind that she would dare fear to be the fastest woman in the track on the earth someday! At the age of nine, against the advice of the doctors, she removed the brace and took the first step the Doctor has said she never would. At age 13, she ran her first race and finished last. At age 15, she went to Tennessee State University where she met a coach by name Ed Temple. She told the coach; "My goal is to become the fastest woman on this planet". The coach replied: **"With your spirit, nobody can stop you".** The summary of the story is that after so many trials, she got into U.S. Olympic team. The little girl who was told she would never walk again on this earth at age four won 100 metres, 200 metres and the 400 metres events of the 1960 Olympics.

No matter what you are going through do not allow fear to steal your faith in God. *Johnson. F. Odesola*

Many of the great men we read about today had it tough when they started, they encountered failure but they never gave up, they kept on trying until success smiled on them.

Henry Ford the inventor of automobile failed and went broke five times before he finally succeeded. It was Henry Wadsworth Longfellow who proclaimed that; **"Into each life, some rain must fell, someday must be dark".** That means no matter how much you try from time to time, your **"sun"** may temporarily disappear. Winston Churchill became a Prime Minister of England at 62 after great struggling and a life time of defeats and setbacks. This great man had framed on the wall of his office the following words: *"I do the very best I can, I mean to keep going. If the end brings me out all right, then what is said against me won't matter. If I am wrong, ten angels swearing I was right won't make a difference."*

Hamilton Marble once affirmed: "Never fear opposition. Kites rise against-not with the wind". Make sure you are right then go ahead. On your way to the top, there is a very noisy and crowded bus stop you must pass through. It is full of PhD (Pull him down) holders and touts! That bus stop is called: **Fear!** Many potential stars/achievers of their generations have "died" and have been "buried" at this bus stop! Be sure you that you are not the next victim! Babe Ruth who is considered by historians to be the greatest athlete of all time, famous for setting the human record in base- ball also holds the record for strike out.

Frank Woolworth who later became a successful business mogul had it rough and tough in the beginning; Frank was so inexperienced that no one really wanted to hire him. Finally he said, "I will work for free just to get some experience", Frank was an outstanding worker, so exciting in his concepts, that he became a multi-millionaire.

The great obstacle to every man's progress is fear. Sometimes it is the failure or crisis of the past that hunts us, thus affecting the present. Many great men who ever accomplished great things in any sphere of life were failures at one time or the other, on one issue or the other. Richard Bach declared that, ***"Every problem has a gift for you in its hands".*** Keep hope alive.

In Nehemiah 6:9; that great builder says, ***"They made us afraid saying their hand shall be weakened from the work".*** Yes, the aim of the enemy sending fear is to weaken you from success. Resist him.

Nancy Anderson said: "Courage is not absence of fear; rather it is the ability to take action in the face of fear". To get to your *Fear of the unknown makes you unknown* Promised Land you need "fearless" spirit. Consider the following nuggets to improve your fearless determination: -

1. **Follow your inner heart conviction**

In the midst of over 6 billion people in the world! Fearlessness means living up to your highest expectation of yourself even if you have to go against popular opinion or tradition. Say "No" when you mean "No" and "Yes" when you mean "Yes." Be distinct in the crowd.

2. **Act courageously**

It is always better to fail in doing something than to excel in doing nothing. Move out of your comfort zone." Dare to do something that causes you to fear and tremble. Fear must be present for courage to be called courage. Take actions that provoke fear! The more you do risky things the more your courage improves! Start now!

3. **Confront something/people**

Concerning a problem or decision, action is king. The more you retreat the more you lose out. Calmly talk to and confront people you have long avoided. Never avoid confronting people in a positive manner. Face them and discover how your courage improves in just few minutes. You need courage to win in life.

Improve on it daily!

The only antidote to fear is faith. Faith is a must for everyone that desires to make it in life.

For God hath not given us the spirit of fear but power and of love and of sound mind (2 Tim 1:7). Fear has conquered many who would have been conquerors, fear has won many who could have been star, fear has subdued many who could have been great, fear has shattered many destinies, rendered useless men of great vision, incapacitated many who would have been successful. It must not do the same to you.

Go ahead and win, go ahead and conquer, make everyday a winning event, you are destined for the top, don't die at the bottom.

Don't forget that Thomas Edison had no formal education! He was sent home after 3 months in School! Steve Wonder was blind! Helen Keller was blind! Lincoln refused to bow to fear of failure and poverty. You are the next to conquer that mountain –Zach 4:7.

Who are thou great mountain before (Your Name) Zerubabel thou shall be made plain.

Fear is a state of the mind, which renders you a prisoner of inertia lacking in ambition. Fear relegates you to the status of a non-achiever, for whom good things just pass by. This mental frame denies you the opportunity to experiment with new ideas that can improve your standard of living. It designates you a captive, unable to think for yourself and must always seek approval from your master fear.

Fear of failure puts you in a permanent state of self–doubt and inadequacy. It destroys your most portent asset; self-confidence. Without self–confidence you will always perform below par. You will always be the object of ridicule among your peers. Your mind will always be crowned with negative thoughts, which can only lead to more failure. To live in fear is to deny yourself of the opportunity to make a difference in this world.

The future generation must look back to your legacy with admiration. You must ignore all protocols of produce and venture into an arsenal of success.

Fear is an enemy of success; if it is allowed in any area of your life it will cripple your faith and end you up as nothing. Break out of every charm of fear into faith.

It is frightening to take risk and try new things, because of fear of failure. We think, what if I fail? What if you do? It will not be your first mistake. No matter how bad it is it probably will not be your worst mistake, neither the last mistake. So the choice is yours to face your fear and defeat it by the help of God.

CHAPTER 13

THE GENTLE TOUCH OF LOVE

"No one cares about me" "I'm so alone"
"I'm different"
"Death would be better for me"

These are some of the things that I hear so often from the people who are a part of my ministration. These are some of the things that I, myself, have sometimes thought and believed and because I know what it feels like to think about these things, my heart shatters in two each and every time someone tells me any one of those things. I so often lay awake at night, trying to find the words I need to convince every person I encounter of their worthiness, of their special purpose for this earth, of how much they really and truly are loved. So many times, I fall asleep, still unsatisfied and frustrated that even as easily as words have always come to me, I cannot seem to find the right ones. The one thing that has so many times, made me feel better is remembering that I'm not alone and so I tell the people I work with, "You're never alone."

But... read that statement: ***"you're never alone."*** It sounds kind of abstract, doesn't it, and difficult to believe when you are in the black of blackness, lonely and afraid. I remember my life and I remember the pain that I had to go through and how lonely I became. I remember how afraid I was. If someone had told me, "you're not alone" I'm not sure I would have believed them. In fact, I may have even thought they were trying to brush me off, patronizing me. Thankfully, I wasn't told, I was *shown* that it *is* the truth.

... lo, I am with you always, even unto the end of the world. Amen. Mathew 28:20

Here is a true life testimony of a beloved child of God: "My sister and I were spending the night with her and we were all three sleeping in the same bed. I don't remember what we were talking about until she said, "If you're ever afraid or can't go to sleep, just hold your hand out, like this" (and she took my wrist and turned it upside down, so that my palm was facing up) "and say a prayer, *Johnson. F. Odesola* asking God to hold your hand. When you do it, you'll feel a warmth like this" (and she placed her other hand over my open palm and I felt a warmth settle over my palm and nodded) - "come over with your hand and you'll know that God is holding it." Curiously, I tried what she said. I held my palm out and I said a prayer.

At this time, I was still very young and so I had the faith of a child and I believed every word I'd been told, so, of course I believed God really would hold my hand. I was right. Minutes after my prayer ended, I felt a soft heat come only over my palm. I stared at my palm in awe and amazement and I curled my fingers in, as I do when I hold someone's hand. The heat stayed with me. I had, up to that point, never experienced so much comfort and peace before in my life. I was young but I knew, lying on that bed, that if God would hold my hand then, He would continue to hold my hand through the trials of my life. I fell asleep that night with my hand on my pillow; palm up, so as to help keep His hand interlocked with mine".

I know it sounds almost silly and difficult to believe, but I *do* believe, with every fibre of my body, that God's hand is holding mine all nights and days. This is the greatest comfort and peace there is because I know, every time that His hand comes down to rest on mine, that all the mistakes I have made and think are so terrible are forgivable in His sight and that because I really believe, everything is all right. Isn't that the kind of love you wish you could have? Unconditional? No matter what mistakes, what terrible things you may do and no matter what the earthly consequences for your actions may be, that there is someone who loves you beyond all measure?

I have news. It's real. And God will hold your hand, just as He is holding mine and He will walk you through the valleys of your life. All you have to do is believe in Him. Sometimes I wonder what happens to all of our childlike faith. I wonder sometimes why it all goes away and when. When does the supernatural ability to believe things we cannot see and to listen to things, which we cannot hear, and to feel things that we cannot touch slip from our grasp? I don't believe it truly ever does. I believe that each of us, somewhere deep inside of us, retains a small piece of that childlike faith and that when we try to find it, it's always there for us, leading us through the rough spots in our lives. In fact, I don't only believe that, I know it to be true, for every time I'm afraid and God takes my hand again, it is proof of his unconditional love.

CHAPTER 14

THE GREATEST RISK IS TO RISK NOTHING

Never resist opportunities and never rehearse impossibilities because today's impossibilities are tomorrow's possibilities! Never review your inadequacies!

Face your inadequacies and look to the Almighty God! Fear not! Try again! Take a risk even once again! Never replace goals with pleasure because of fear! Never reject the personal cost of your goals! Never resist change even if you can! Never allow procrastination or fear to keep you from any necessary step.

One of the pioneers of aviation in the world Charles Lindbergh once emphasized that 'What kind of man would live where there is no daring? I don't believe in talking foolish changes, but nothing can be accomplished if we do not take any chance at all.

You may have delays, disappointments or limited success, only risk takers are high flyers on this planet earth. You must know that throughout history, men like Christopher Columbus, Crocket Lewis, Henry Ford, and the Wright Brothers who became pioneers were risk takers! William Channing said: ***"There are periods when to dare is the highest wisdom"***. Decide to risk, decide to pray, decide to trust God again! Decide to invest your money again! Decide to write the examination again! Decide to still trust in people's ability again!

Sidney Harris said: ***"Regret for the things we did can be tempered by time: It is regret for the things we did not do that is inconsolable"***. If you take risks and fail, you will have fewer regrets than if you do nothing and fail! Dick Butler advice people as they prepare to get into new height that: "Life isn't fair! Isn't going to be fair! Stop wishing and whining and go out and make it happen for you". You may be taking greatest risk to risk nothing! The reality is that everything in life is risk! Romans 14:23; *".…. Whatsoever is not of faith is sin":* Hebrews 11:6 …. *"Without faith it is impossible to please God".*

Let God see your step of faith and watch your borders enlarge! Wishing that a risk wasn't yours to take won't make it easier! There is nothing so fatiguing as the external hanging of an uncompleted task! A risk is not a foolish action; if you want to avoid all risks, then don't ride in motorcars or buses because they cause 20% of all fatal accidents. Or don't travel by air, rail, or water because they cause 6%*Johnson. F. Odesola* of all accidents! Or don't walk on the streets because 15% of all accidents occur there! Or don't stay at home because 17% of all accidents happen there! But is that possible? No! Resist fear! G.K. Chesterton said: "I do not believe in a fate that falls on men however, they act, but I do believe in fate that falls on them unless they act". Isaiah 60:1; Says:

> *Arise, shine; for thy light is come, and the glory of the LORD is risen upon thee*

You cannot shine till you arise (take an action). The less you venture out, the greater your risk of failure. The more you risk failure and actually fail, the greater your chances of success. I would rather try something great and fail than try nothing great and succeed. If you take four steps forward and one step backwards you have made progress? Little progress is better than no progress at all! The world is waiting to celebrate you!

One Chinese proverb says: *"Be not afraid of going slowly; be only afraid of standing still".* A.T. Williams said: "All you can do is all you can do, but all you can do is not enough".

The size of your success is determined by the size of your belief. The size of your belief is also the size of the risk involved to succeed.

There is this story of certain travellers who were crossing a desert location on a Carmel Caravan. After about three days' journey, they came across a signpost, which reads: "Pick up some pebbles and put them in your pockets". Travel a day's journey and look at the pebbles. You will be both glad and sad. Moved by this sign, the curious travellers picked some pebbles inquisitively!

Some others ignored what they called 'the stupid post in the wildernesses! To their surprise, the pebble had turned into Gold nuggets! The signpost was correct: They were both glad and sad! Glad they had picked up a few pebbles, but sad that they hadn't picked up a whole lot more! Others were sad because they didn't pick any! They wished they had picked or even more!

Wayne Dyer asked a fundamental question "Man's reach should exceed his grasp or what's a heaven for?" Don't forget that: "No better is good enough where best is possible". Stretch your faith; take a risk again!

Take a good look at what is left of your life and decide to make it count. Life is the saddest words that are found on a tombstone that reads: **"When it came time to die, I had not lived".** It is *The greatest risk is to risk nothing* frightening to take risks and try new things. We think, "What if I fail?" "What if you do"? It will not be your first mistake. And no matter how bad it is, it probably will not be your worst mistake. And unless you fail at something really spectacular like attempting to climb Mount Kilimanjaro or swim the Indian Ocean, it probably will not be your last mistake.

One thing you can count on, whichever way it goes you will grow in wisdom, experience and character. In other words you will become wiser for just having tried. Rick warren writes:

> *"I could have taken a hundred gifts and abilities tested as a young man and would never have discovered that I was gifted at teaching, because I had never done it! It was only after I began accepting opportunities to speak that I saw the results, received confirmation from others and realized God has gifted me to do this".*

Unless you are willing to risk getting involved, you are not going to know what you are good at. The road to success is never mistake – free. But then, neither is the road to failure. So the choice is yours. That is why Paul wrote "Make a careful exploration of who you are and the work you have been given and then sink yourself into (Galatians 6:4 NIV). No risk, no reward!

Nothing good in this world has ever been achieved without risk. Neither in Science nor Arts! Everything around us was achieved because someone took it upon himself/herself to the risky lonely route of discovery. The daring spirit enabled us to look at our present circumstances and declared them inadequate, then actually sought to improve upon them. The daring mind propelled Thomas Edison to discover the bulb; otherwise we would be still plunged in darkness!

People who lack daring spirit stop growing, show me someone who is not effective, I will show you someone who has not risked learning anything new. ***You are what you are; you are where you are, because of the risk you have not taken.*** Go for the biggest! Why not? That is what the big achievers do. Big achievers take on bigger tasks. They take risks. They go the longer route. They assigned themselves more responsibilities. They climb taller mountain not "tinny hills". They feel challenged by obstacles placed in their way and go on to overcome them.

At the end of it all, they are well grounded, polished and eager to take on even bigger risks. All the best things happened because someone bit off more than they could chew. They set greater challenges to prove their abilities.

Burst all odds and move on! Barry Lumping was 26 when a rare liver disease sent him into the world of silence. He became deaf, unable to pursue his chosen carrier, he could not bail out a strife – torn marriage, settle for being a popular parent instead of a godly one, stay home and watch TV instead of going to Church or not bother sharing your faith.

Every day you must choose between doing what is right or what is convenient; living by your convictions or compromising for the sake of greed and approval: taking a risk or staying in your comfort zone. In other words, you must decide between trusting God (even when you do not understand his ways), or living in doubt and second – guessing him.

Abraham journeyed up Mount Moriah to sacrifice the son he loved more than his own life. Genesis 22: 1-2; "...God tested Abraham's (faith and obedience). God's test will stretch you to your limits! They will demand every ones of courage you have got and risk. But you cannot have a testimony without a test! Just like God told Moses by the red sea: "Move on". He will give you strength to equal the test or challenge! The road may be rough and the enemy powerful but remember; God *"goes before you ... (and) will not... forsake you".*

Caleb is the Champion of the second half. Hear him: "Give me this Hill country, even though I am Eighty–five. I am strong as I was at forty". (Paraphrased Joshua 14:7–12 TLB). Caleb probably said this in front of a score of young men murmuring for easy assignments when it came to occupying the Promised Land. The hill country was full of walled cities and giants. Who wanted that? The old man did. May be your life has not been too impressive to date. You did not do a great job raising your children, you squandered a marriage, follow second–class priorities and now regret it. Do not stay there too long. Take a risk again. We serve a God who can redeem our mistakes! E. Stanley Jones writes: "There are scars on my faith, but underneath those scars there are no doubts. (Christ) has me with all the consent of my being. I'm 83, and I'm more excited today about being a Christian than I was at 18, when I first put my feet upon this way!" Hey, get back in the race and start running with God, running stumble-free does not make you The *greatest risk is to risk nothing* winner, finishing strong does!

> Mathew 25:29; (NKJ) says: ***For unto every one that hath shall be given, and he shall have abundance: but from him that hath not shall be taken away even that which he hath.***

Can there be any more powerful incentive of godly risk taking than Jesus' parable of the talents? Three men were given money to invest. Two invested wisely and multiplied theirs. The third had his because he was afraid to risk and fail. To him the Master said, ***"You wicked and lazy servant……… you ought to have deposited my money ….and…. I would have received Back……. with interest".*** **(Mathews 25:14-30)**. Understand this good stewardship requires thoughtful risk-taking.

But what if I fail? Failure trains you for success! It can actually show you what you need to change as you move forward and attempt next venture. As God's people we have a security net beneath us that allows us to fail safely. However, if our self-worth is all tied up in knots around some failed enterprise, then we will not be motivated to try again.

It is human nature to try to feel good, to succeed, to win the prize, to move forward and not backwards. But like a world–class athlete backing up so that he can run faster, jump higher or throw further, sometimes we must accept that a few backwards steps now, can fuel our progress later. Accept risk–taking now so that you can rejoice in the success that comes later.

CHAPTER 15

IF YOU WON'T STOP WORRYING YOU WON'T SUFFERING

Build your self – confidence by wiping away worry. Your confidence cannot be built until worry is destroyed from your life. Worry is a feeling or an expression of anxiety. Many situations exists that make men anxious, some are real while a majority are simply magnified – that is, what men conjure up in their minds. Studies from psychologists give the following statistics about what people worry most about.

- 40% of the worries are about things that never happened
- 30% are past events that man cannot change
- 10% are petty and miscellaneous worrying i.e. Needless worries that carry no weight.
- 12% of the worries are about health
- 8% of people's worries are real.

From the statistics it's clear that 99% of what people worry about are unchangeable. Further research shows that 30% of people are non-worriers, 15% are chronic worriers while the rest, 55% fall in between the first mentioned two groups. Some of us think it is legitimate to worry. However, no matter what you think about it, it adds to your problem instead of solving it.

Worry is a sin that does not only destroy a man's health but also leads to death. Philippians 4:6 stated:

Be careful for nothing; but in everything by prayer and supplication with thanksgiving, let your requests be made known unto God.

Someone said: Worry, like a locking chain will give you something to do but it will not get you anywhere. God has the final word about our worries He says in Mathew 6:25:

Therefore I say unto you, Take no thought for your life, what ye shall eat, or what ye shall drink; nor yet for your body, what ye shall put on. Is not the life more than meat, and the body than raiment?*If you won't stop worrying you won't suffering*

Remember that behind every worry there is an element of doubt and lack of faith in God. Why worry when you can pray? So do not worry or be anxious about tomorrow, for tomorrow will have worries and anxieties of its own. Sufficient for each day is its own trouble. Has it dawned on you that today was the tomorrow of yesterday. There are two days in every week in which you must never worry. In fact there are just two days which should be kept free from anxiety, worry and fear over the future or concern over the past. The two days are ***"Yesterday and today"*** and *"**tomorrow"***, yesterday with all its mistakes and cares, failures faults and blunders, pain or arches has gone forever beyond control. All the money in the world cannot bring back yesterday.

You cannot undo a single act you performed yesterday nor erase a single word you said. So forget it and move on. If you die because of the past, then you have murdered "a great star".

The other day you must never worry about is ***"Tomorrow"*** with all its possible adversity, its burdens and fear. Tomorrow also is beyond your immediate control. Never Forget that the sun will rise in splendour behind a mask of cloud; it must rise but until it does you have no stake in the tomorrow. You cannot play God. Stop that peeping into your tomorrow. There is only ***"Alpha and Omega"***. He is the only one who is qualified to look into the tomorrow because He is the creator of the tomorrow. Bind fear, bind anxiety. The tomorrow you fear will come out to prove your fear as unreal. This leaves you with only one day - **today.** Is it not true that it is the experience of **today** that drives a person mad? It is the remorse or bitterness about something which happened yesterday and the dread (strong fear) of what tomorrow will bring. Therefore, live a day at a time. A man who was about to die left the following words for his son: **My son I have worried all my life and nine- tenth of the things I worry about never come to pass.** Avoid the mistake of this dying father. One of the greatest enemies of the human race is worry.

According to *John Haggi's* comments on the United State of America, he said mental unrest cost America two and half billion dollars a year. More Americans commit suicide than die from any of the five most common communicable diseases. For instance in 1957 220 people died of polio, 15980 committed suicide, 7500 more people committed suicide than were victims of human homicide. A total of 10, 170 people died as a result of ulcers, at least 17 million *Johnson. F. Odesola*

Americans are suffering from some form of mental illness. During the Second World War, more than 300 000 of American young men were killed in combat. During the same period over one million civilians died from heart attack mainly because of worry. You can imagine more people die from worry-related sickness than any other killer disease.

A doctor said that worry causes heart trouble, high blood pressure, asthma, ulcer, arthritis, migraine, headaches, thyroid malfunction and rheumatism.

Refuse to worry! It never solves any problem, rather it complicate issues. Handle each day's problems. Forget the past. Ignore tomorrow. It is in God's hand. It is when you and I add the burdens of the two awful eternities – yesterday and tomorrow that we break down. Today's victory is guaranteed by the grace of God. Today's cares are in the engine room of our creator already. Today's problems can handle themselves because of what Isaiah 49: 43 say

> *Thus saith the Lord GOD, Behold, I will lift up mine hand to the Gentiles, and set up my standard to the people: and they shall bring thy sons in their arms, and thy daughters shall be carried upon their shoulders.*

Deuteronomy 33:27 also affirmed that;

> ***The eternal God is thy refuge, and underneath are the
> everlasting arms: and he shall thrust out the enemy from before
> thee; and shall say, Destroy them.***

God is a loving Father and helper. His job is to throw out the enemy.
If you have prayed over any matter then you must relax because the
battle is the Lord's. When you worry you are taking over the battle, the
automatic consequences are shame, stagnation, demotion and avoidable
death. Roger Barret says: ***Worry is a wretched experience that leaves you
exhausted, uninvolved and in- deep hopeless despair: you feel doomed,
trampled …it is awful.*** Dr Charles Mayo adds that, ***Worry affects
circulation; the glands; the whole nervous system and profoundly
affects the heart.*** George Lyon wrote: ***Worry is the interest paid by those
who borrow trouble.*** Why do you want to borrow trouble by worrying?.
Mr. Disney told his staff: ***"Why worry? If you have done the very best
you can or failed the worst you can, worry won't make it better."*** *If you
won't stop worrying you won't suffering*

Live a day at a time! Crowd out the emotion of worry and instil in its
place enthusiasm, positive thinking and personal self- confidence.

A frustrated woman whose new car was stolen snapped angrily at
her husband. ***"How can you joke about this when our brand new car
is missing"?*** The husband looked at her and said: ***"Honey, we can have
a stolen car and all we can do is be upset or we can have a stolen car
and be happy. Either way we have a stolen car".*** His comments sent
her thinking and she avoided further tension. The deed of what happened
to you has been done. Your crying or feeling depressed cannot bring the
victory. Do not forget that African common bitter leaf produces sweetness
in meals. It is when singing goes that murmuring sign in. That you are
alive at all should cause you to be excited daily. That you failed in the past
does not mean you will fail again.

Determine to re – define your past, even if you cannot rectify it, see it as a
necessary bus stop to your destination. Avoid depression because it wounds the
spirit *(Proverb 17:22).* Always bear in mind that until you are depressed you

cannot be oppressed or suppressed. All your carry over will be carried down in Jesus name. Victory is sweetest when you have known defeat. (Malcolm Forbes). ***Declare your hope daily in God. Smile and look younger!*** You can either read History or make History. Make your life an exclamation and not explanation. Make your life authentic and not just synthetic.

Stop looking sad, cheated and defeated. Despite the past maltreatment and hurts of Joseph he forgot his past. Why do you think his boss, Potiphar, was so relaxed and left everything under his charge? Why was Mrs. Potipha lusting after Joseph? Because the young man was not looking sad, dry depressed or sick. He conquered his past and was looking fresh, relaxed and handsome because he was excited about where he was going. You can also do the same.

I once read how fire destroyed the business of Sir. Thomas Ava Edison on December 9th, 1914. The terrible and traumatic loss was well over $2million. In that fire most of the scientific research were burnt to ashes. The second bad news for him was that his insurance was only $238. The third bad news was that the man was close to the biblical fruitful age of 70 years. He was 67 years. Immediately after the fire, Edison went to the site of sorrow and made an amazing statement: ***"There is great value in disaster. All our mistakes are Johnson. F. Odesola*** burnt ***up. Thank God we can start again".*** So in facing the reality, it means all he had worked for in 67 years was burnt but this man rose from the past calamity to become a cerebrated scientist/genius. Exactly three weeks after that disaster, Edison and his crew produced the first Phonograph (early from disc player – modern CD player) in history. ***Truly, it is only mad men that can excel in this mad world.***

Therefore refuse to be moved by the thought of your age, past delay or unanswered prayers. The road to success is dotted with many empty packing spaces. Don't make your disappointment or disaster your packing space in your life's journey. Keep moving when the world says *"Give up,"* hope whispers, *"try it once more time." Jason Gracian* says; ***"Life feels long and passes quickly. Don't be fooled. Get out there and start packing more life into what time you have"*** The 6th US President, John Quincy Adams wrote; ***"Patience and perseverance have magical effects before which difficulties disappear and obstacles vanish".*** George F Tiltonood was right when he said: ***Success is never final and failure never fatal, it is courage that counts.***

You must make a quality decision to turn your flaw into a flower. A water bearer in India had two large pots he carried on each end of a pole across his neck from the local stream to his master's house. Unfortunately he was only delivering one and a half pot content because one the pots had a crack and were always leaking off the water before he got home. Of course, the perfect pot was proud of its accomplishments, since it was perfectly fulfilling the purpose for which it was made. But the cracked pot was ashamed of its imperfections and failures. It said to its owner at the stream one day: "This crack on my side has made your housework burdensome. You do not get full value for your efforts and your boss constantly harasses you. I am ashamed of myself." The water bearer then replied; "As we return home I want you to notice all the beautiful flowers along the path. You will see that there are flowers only in your side of the path and not on the other pot's side. I noticed the crack and decided to turn it into an advantage by planting flower seeds on your side of the path and every day while we walk from the stream, you've watered them for two years. I use these beautiful flowers to decorate my master's table. "Without your being the way you are, he would not have this beauty to grace his house". God can turn the present disappointment disaster or past failure into a fortune and He can turn the flaws into flowers. Never *If you won't stop worrying you won't suffering* you condemn yourself or pity yourself. God can turn your mistake into a miracle. God is perfecting everything that concerns you and making all things work for your good.

An old legend told of an angel who was sent by God to tell Satan that all his method to defeat his children would be taken from him. The devil pleaded to keep just one; ***"Let me retain depression/worry"***. The angel thinking this is a small request agreed. "Good", Satan exclaimed. He laughed and said: ***"In that one gift I have secured all"***. Truly legends are fables and not real stories, but they are powerful life teaching tools. A man had a box where each time he had worry he'd write it down and deposit it in the box. Then on one faithful day in which he had worried he tried to read the context of his worry box. Surprisingly, he found out most of the things he had worried about had already been resolved or they never happened. In anger and sensing deception by worry, he set the box on fire. Worry is Satan's double barrel tool.

In times of stress, force yourself to be cheerful; Proverb 17:22 says;

> *A merry heart doeth good like medicine, but broken spirit dries the bones*

Take note that whatever can dry your bones can take your life. Worry and anxiety concerning any matter can end up taking your life! Since you do not have a solution to some of the problems you are going through, is it not wisdom to take life easy and deal with issues step by step by waiting on the Lord? (Isaiah 44:23)

> *Sing, O ye heavens; for the LORD hath done it: shout, ye lower parts of the earth: break forth into singing, ye mountains, O forest, and every tree therein: for the LORD hath redeemed Jacob, and glorified himself in Israel.*

Hear what Dr Charles Moyo said; *"I have never seen a man who died of overwork but many who died from stress".* Trials are compulsory for anyone destined for the top. This problem will pass away and end up for your total good. Apply the weapon of self- control. Self-control is the balance wheel that directs your action and leads you to be positive and prayerful and overcome the destructiveness of worry. Worry always destroys! Cloud it out with enthusiastic action: Maintain an atmosphere of laughter.

CHAPTER 16

CONVERSATION VS CONFRONTATION

Imagine a father, enraged by some little incident that occurred within the home earlier in the day. He was so angry with the hand that life has dealt him that when his wife slaps him across the cheek, he hits her back. Imagine a mother, so heartbroken because of the things that her husband does to her and her children, that, in the heat of anger, she takes a drawer full of his clothes and throws them into the fireplace. Imagine a young, ten year old boy sitting beside his heartbroken mother, knowing the mother was hurting and yet not knowing what to say to alleviate the pain of this broken mother. All he can do is sit there, unable to say the things that might comfort the mother and yet unwilling to let his mother alone in pain. And imagine that little boy laying on his bed, curled into a fetal position, tears on his cheeks, his hands curled tight around a fistful of bed sheet, listening to his parents sling accusations at each other.

The scenes that you've just imagined were part of many daily lives. Fighting between parents is really the only memory they have of them together. Rarely can they picture them laughing or talking while complete peace reigned in the air. Many grew up knowing with a certainty that they could feel that their mother loved the so called father and yet very often being left uncertain about what exactly the father felt. They were never quite sure if it was genuine love for them, or the need for attention that continued bringing him home from his unexpected and unexplained trips away from family. And the fights were never explained either.

What do you think of such a boy who is an adult now, and entering relationships of their own? Such would be too "passive" and "give in too easily" and "over sensitive", whenever a voice is raised or tension enters the air.

It is easy to tell the people that entered your life, to cry for help, "There is a reason for everything and one day you will look back on the things you're going through with new understanding" but do you really believe it yourself, because there are certain "events" in my own life that I never really thought that I would ever gain understanding nor would there ever be a reason good enough to explain it all away. However, Romans 8:28 says;*Conversation Vs Confrontation*

> *And we know that all things work together for good to them that love God, to them who are the called according to his purpose.*

Here is what I thought, based on my knowledge of God's instructions. With the maturity that only time and the chance to live in relative peace brings, we need to be able to re-evaluate our childhood and life experience with clearer realization of the valuable lesson they have to offer.

Raising voices and fists, getting angry and shouting to get the point across resolves nothing. All it does is temporarily soothe the sometimes powerful need to tell the other person exactly what you think of their actions or words. It does not help the situation. I know beyond a shadow of a doubt that people are even more wounded after a fight, physical and verbal, than what they started out with. Before any confrontation, you are hurt because of an action and you felt abandoned, neglected, or betrayed and keeping those feelings inside of you made things worse to the point of explosion. When your anger explodes and within minutes, a fight had erupted, words would be spoken, accusations made, and tears were shed until the truth of the original disagreement would get lost in the need to inflict as much emotional pain on each other.

When this occurs, I mean this need for revenge and the need to see the other person hurt and degraded, takes over, nothing is said that is of any good because it's probably not even true. From this point on, words become weapons of revenge, not tools of communication, and the disagreement becomes worthless. Nothing is resolved and when the dust clears and the fists come down and the accusations stop, the pain is still there and more comes to the heart because of the new emotional wounds inflicted by the argument. The end result, therefore, seems to defeat the purpose of the original confrontation, doesn't it?

The original purpose, of course, was to resolve an issue, to finally make peace about something that had been bothering you for some time. Instead, all that is accomplished when anger gets in the way is more pain and more issues that will probably be dealt with eventually with a new fight, which will bring about new issues to be dealt with later and so on and so on... In addition to having to deal with the new issues brought about by words that were spoken in the heat of anger, the original issue still remains unresolved. The cycle is vicious, never ending and it affects everyone involved: not only *Johnson. F. Odesola* the two fighting.

Because of my view and because of the apprehension I have of raised voices, I made a conscious choice not to ever engage in a verbal fight or clash. To have a calm discussion about the things that are upsetting me is an acceptable way of dealing with pain that may be inside me. This accomplishes its purpose, usually: to bring to me understanding and then acceptance of an action performed or a statement made. What I would do to help this world realize that a conversation helps to heal so many wounds and in a more peaceful manner than raised voices ever has or ever will.

God wants us to talk about our problems: holding them inside of us is dangerous. It's like a boiling pot. If you put a pot of water on the stove, and cover it, then eventually, it's going to start to boil and sizzle and if you don't take the lid off of it, then soon, it will burst throwing the lid off itself. But, if you take the lid off before that happens, then it will sizzle down itself and will not result in an eruption. We work the same way. If we hold things, bad things, inside of us, then eventually, we'll burst and an argument will break out: we'll explode. Or the consequences may be worse than that, in that we may choose to harm ourselves. But if we talk about those feelings calmly, and invite God in to help us deal with them, then the bad feelings will slowly and smoothly disappear. We need to *talk* about our problems but we don't need to shout and use fists and anger to try to resolve a conflict.

In his approximately 30 years of life, Christ is only recorded to have been angry one time: one time in a lifetime! That's a pretty good example to try and follow, isn't it? My father's philosophy that says, "If you are wronged, then you have the right to express your feelings to the one who wronged you" is correct. You are special and worthy: you have the right and you need to let others know when they have hurt you, but why not learn of more peaceful ways of doing that so that you may find resolution rather than resorting to angry, hurtful and often untrue words that only begin a cycle of more pain for you? *There is a better way to solve your problems*

Remember, it is conversation *not* confrontation that is the stepping stone to healing

CHAPTER 17

INFORMATION IS THE MIDWIFE
OF REFORMATION

Everyone called great are great because they are readers. Knowledge is not a gift it is consciously acquired through diligent study and research. Develop your reading scheme.

Make studying a culture. Make it a life style. Make it a hobby, 2 Timothy 2:15; says:

> *Study to shew thyself approved unto God, a workman that needeth not to be ashamed, rightly dividing the word of truth.*

The late American President, John F Kennedy was able to digest an amazing amount of reports because he could read 1,200 words a minute. He literally had developed his reading rate to a phenomenal amount.

Until you are diligent reader you cannot be approved in the school of the achievers. The diligent will be intelligent. The intelligent man is always open to new ideas. In fact look for them (Proverbs 18:15TLB). One idea can change everything!

Bill Gates had an idea but when he went looking for investors some of his big-money friends called it "too risky". Can you imagine how they feel now? Good ideas are great.

God's ideas are even better! You see, what God initiates, he backs up with resources of heaven. (Philippians 4:19 KJV) Said: *But my God shall supply all your need according to his riches in glory by Christ*

Jesus. Imagine being empowered by God and underwritten by the Bank of heaven!

God's problem has never been lack of ideas; it is finding people who will leave their comfort zone and act on them like the father of faith (Abraham), who, ***"By faith...when called to go ...... went, even though he did not know where he was going"*** (Hebrews 11:8).

And what was his reward? ***"........all the families of the earth will be blessed through you ...."*** (Genesis 28:14: NIV).

Usually God gives us His ideaswhen:

(a) Ours failed.

(b) We have laid aside our pre-conditions and we are willing to do whatever He says.*Johnson. F. Odesola*

(c) We are willing to risk.

(d) We are committed to giving Him all the glory.

Think what one of God's ideas could do for your life, business, family and ministry. ***"........what I have said, that I will bring about, what I have planned, that will I do"*** (Isaiah 46:11 NIV).

God's already spoken certain things over your life. Seek him by study and he will reveal them to you! To have the knowledge of your assignment on this side of the planet, then you need information, which can only be acquired by intensive study. If you are adequately informed about the knowledge of your assignment and you understand people, great opportunities abound for you.

When Bill Gates was 11 years old he won a competition put up by his Pastor. The competition was that everyone should memorize Mathew 5, 6 and 7 and quote it as accurately as possible. Bill at that tender age was the only one who could quote it perfectly well without any mistake at all. His Pastor, wanting to know his secret, called him and asked him; "how did you do it?" He answered with the kind of confidence anyone would have mustered, "I can do anything if I put my mind to it".

At age 8, he had finished reading the encyclopaedia. Before he was 13, each time they were given assignments in school, while his other classmates wrote four or five pages, Bill would write more than 30 pages. At the age of 19 Bill Gates started MICROSOFT with his friends. At age 24, he was already a millionaire, at this same age he sat to do business with the most

Senior I.B.M. Executives. He became a billionaire at 31 and less than 10 years later he became the richest man in the world.

Acquire knowledge, let your brain sweat, it will in turn bring you sweet blessings.

Read books of inspiration. Read autobiographies, read biographies. Read books of faith, read motivational books and magazines. Much more than other books, read the Bible, the greatest book of all times.

A father was approached by his small son, who told him proudly, *"I know what the Bible means!"* His father smiled and replied, *"What do you mean, you 'know' what the bible means".* The son replied, *"I do know!" "Ok"*, said the father! *"So son what does the Bible means?" "That is easy, Daddy. It stands for Basic Information Before leaving Earth".* The Bible contains the vitamins for healthy soul. *Information is the midwife of reformation*

Have a functioning library – spend money on books because you are a total sum of what you know. Never allow a day to roll by without acquiring a fresh knowledge. Be addicted to books and success will be addicted to you.

Be the best in your field, read books and magazines that can help you to be more efficient in your field. You have only one life to live and it must not be wasted. The difference between a rut and a grave is only a matter of inches.

It takes insight to gain height. You need insight to reign. Great men that have influenced our generation are men that are sold out to books. Without extra knowledge you cannot have extra success and achievement. Daniel became great through books: he lived a life of distinction and total success! In Daniel 9:2 we have this attestation that:

> *In the first year of his reign I Daniel understood by books the number of the years, whereof the word of the LORD came to Jeremiah the prophet, that he would accomplish seventy years in the desolations of Jerusalem.*

Without books your destiny cannot be a reality. You need to acquire knowledge to fulfil your destiny. *"You cannot be made alone you need*

people who have gone ahead" to live ahead. You need appropriate books to live appropriate life. Gather motivational books and brainstorm yourself with them, load yourself until you become loaded for success.

Being busy will want to keep you from study; anything that keeps you away from study has deprived you of your success. Laziness and procrastination will want to keep you from breakthrough. John Milton, a British poet wrote: ***"He who reigns within himself and rules passions, desires and fears is more than a king"***. Discipline yourself. Mark Twain wrote that: "Twenty years from now, you will be more disappointed by the things that you didn't do than by the ones you did do. So, throw off the lowliness and sail away from the safe harbour. Catch the trade winds in your sails".

Take time to read materials that matters to your destiny, don't just read any book, read inspiring books only, real motivational books that can motivate you and launch you into the success. Life is a journey; you need the right materials or books to end up in the *Johnson. F. Odesola* right destination.

Load your brain with unbeatable stuff; it will in turn give you the dividend tomorrow.

Failure and redundancy has become my eternal enemies because I am addicted to motivational books; inspirational books are my daily companions. I read everyday to the level that the day says Bravo! That is one of the major secrets of life success.

Wake up with books and sleep with books, you will soon become an envy of your world. Your destiny is not in the hands of any man: It is in your hands. You can sharpen your destiny through nooks. Read relevant books to live a relevant life.

You cannot walk in the path of the common men and yet desire an outstanding result. You must discipline yourself to study; you also need to discipline your thoughts before you can be enlisted amongst rare breed of men walking in the path of uncommon success.

Men of uncommon success are men of total distinction; they made up their minds to study their way to greatness and earned a great destiny.

CHAPTER 18

TOO MANY EXPECTATIONS

Many throughout their entire life are known as the "good boy." Such people will say: I always get good grades in school and now in college, teachers and professors love me, I never get into trouble and never have. I was the "quiet" and the "good" child. I was praised at a very young age for my "good manners" and my smile, and if I ever were to do something wrong, it was as if I had just irreversibly shocked and disappointed my entire family.

As I grew older, I developed very irrational and yet equally real fears of disappointing my family. I knew that my parents were not too okay with their finances and I was always terrified of adding to their problems. And if I knew that a member of my family was hurting or angry I took the blame for the problem because I would much rather have the blame be placed on me rather than have them angry at one another. Sometimes, I even invented crazy tales about *how* certain things, which I had not even been a part of, were my fault. And I hid behind a masked smile and an automatic "I'm fine" reply to those people who asked if I was okay.

Eventually, the pressure to be "perfect" and to live up to all the expectations that I felt were placed on me and which I placed on myself became too great for me to handle and I began to do things to myself that were detrimental to my health. I did not care. In perfect honesty, I didn't even realize it because, by that time, I had become so focused on maintaining harmony in my home and among my friends and being "Mr Perfect" that my feelings were buried and I didn't even realize that I was acting in seriously harmful ways towards myself.

I thought everyone was looking to me to keep their world in balance. I suppose now it was somewhat a selfish thought because intellectually we all know that one person cannot hold together everyone else's life. My friend brought it to my attention one day when he attempted to rub my shoulders and realized that I was incapable of relaxing. "Hey, listen," he said, smiling to take the truth and the sting out of his words, "I know it's hard for us to believe but the world will be okay if you take a moment and stop holding it together." He is the first person, and the only person (or so I believed) in my life that has never expected me to be perfect. When I make a mistake (and I make hundreds of them) he talks to me about it and then. ... It's over. He doesn't treat me any differently than he ever has.

A lot of us think that the people in our worlds expect certain things from us. They expect us to be perfect, to never fail and to always be calm and collected. At least, that's what we think. But you know what? I don't believe that's true.

We are our own harshest critics: no one else expects as much out of us as we ourselves do. If we can come to believe this is true then we can start living more joyful and fulfilling lives. When we have so many expectations on us and feel as though we must be perfect to be loved (which isn't true at all) then every day seems to be a duty, an obligation, rather than a privilege. Some say, "I work best under pressure" and that may very well be true. I am among those who do. But just because our work is the best then doesn't necessarily mean that that's when we're at our happiest.

Life, in my opinion, has too many good surprises that we'll miss if we only concern ourselves with reaching perfection. Not only that, but no one knows better than ourselves do that we fail constantly. Flawlessness is not attainable: we will not go one day without doing something we should not do because we are human and so when we fail, if we are perfectionists, then we must live daily with guilt for not making that A or not being able to accomplish whatever we felt we should have.

Guilt is without a shadow of a doubt the hardest emotion to face, so if we could look at ourselves and what we expect out of ourselves more honestly and realistically then some of our guilt could be diminished, leaving room for more happiness and joy.

Ephesians 1:11 TM

"In Christ .... we find out who we are and what we are living for ......"

Sarah Breathnach says: "perfectionism has many aliases. Getting it right ..... fixing it ... revising it.... tinkering .... having high standards. However, it has really nothing to do with [those] things. Perfectionism is a refusal to let yourself move ahead. It's an obsessive debilitating closed system that causes you to get stuck ... a pursuit of the worst in ourselves, the part that tell us nothing we do will ever be good enough!"

The media and entertainment industry spend millions daily bombarding us with impossible images of airbus perfection. They make you think you should be thinner, smarter, better than anything other than who God made you to be. Looking around, all you see are people who seem happier, wiser and richer. It's as if they *Too many expectations* know the secret and you don't. Galatians 1:10

"... do I seek to please men? for if I yet pleased men, I should not be the servant of Christ".

A talented young musician studies under a famous violin teacher. Now it was time for his first recital! He performed magnificently and received numerous 'bravos'! Strangely he seems not to hear them, but kept glancing anxiously at the front row. It wasn't until a white-haired man rose and nodded graciously, that the young violinist started smile. His master had praised his work! He has received the only approval that matters! Whose approval do you seek? Be honest! It is important to know how far you are willing to go in order to win the praise of others or let their opinions influence you. Our purpose is to please [Him], not people. Tavis Smiley says: ***"Take your focus off how others see you. Cease being obsessed with the need to impress. Don't allow the approval of others to obstruct your view of yourself".*** Remember, any time you set goals, establish boundaries or change old patterns, you are going to get criticism from those who are used to you behaving in a certain way. Have your courage and convictions. Do not let that stop you from doing what you know is right!

Changing our belief patterns and our expectations is very difficult but it can be done. Use the determination that helps you to accomplish so much perfection to say, "I'm not going to worry today. I'm going to go to the park and enjoy myself". Write a list that lists all the good things about yourself and that will help you balance your mistakes with your achievements. Talk about your emotions and fears to someone. I promise you, they would much rather you tell them how you really feel than for you to harm yourself, as I did. Surround yourself with friends that you feel comfortable with and that you don't feel as though you have to impress. And remember that God knew you were going to fail often and He still created you. He still loves you! Relax and enjoy the gifts of life rather than attacking it. You're loved just by opening your eyes each morning. ***You don't have to be perfect to be loved.***

Do you know that by constantly putting yourself down you are insulting your Maker? In His eyes you are "just right". He never makes anything that is not! So if you are struggling in the endless quest for perfection, make this your prayer: 'Father, You are my Maker, my Sustainer, my Rewarder. You are also the Lover of my soul. In spite of my limitations and struggles I thank you for the work you have done and will continue to do in me. Help me to honour you by loving and accepting myself the way you do! In Jesus' Name, Amen

CHAPTER 19

SIGNIFICANCE OF FRIENDSHIP

Amos 3:3: ***Can two walk together, except they be agreed?***

If asked, we would all probably agree that having friends is very important and not only is important, but it's usually fun, right? I mean, we have the opportunity to talk about the latest progress, events and places we like, we get to go to, do things with our friends, they make us laugh and feel special and accepted.

But is that what being friends is all about? Chatting about relationships and laughing? Or does being a friend mean something else, too – does it carry special responsibilities? I think that when we say that we're a friend to someone, then we need to do all we can to help make sure our friend is safe and happy. Being a friend, to me, means asking if our friends are okay and genuinely trying to help them through tough times.

One of the hardest parts of being a friend is being sworn to secrecy and then being told something that our friends are being deliberately hurt by someone (such as being abused or a secret affliction) or that they are choosing to do something that is dangerous to themselves (such as drugs or something else). We've sworn not to tell but our hearts know that the situation they are in is bad and dangerous.

What do we do?

We don't want to risk having them get angry at us and ending the friendship and yet it's tough going through each day knowing that they are being raped or hit or turning to cocaine or ecstasy. We don't want to lose their trust or make it a bigger deal than it may be really is but we also don't want to wonder about whether or not our choice to remain silent is the right one. From everything in my life, to all the troubles I have heard from other people, I can say that true friends find the courage to talk, to reveal those dangerous secrets in such moments.

Whether they are aware of it or not, people who tell friends about the serious situations they are in, are asking for help. People who do drugs usually do not try to hide that fact from anyone but the police and their parents. Their friends, though, usually know that they are on drugs. The friend who told the others the situation did so because they really want help.

Why don't they come out and say they need help, then?

It's kind of hard to grasp, but people who are in dangerous situations often don't really believe anyone cares about them and/or they don't believe that they can be helped. It may also be that they are afraid of having their parents find out the truth. Sometimes when we're really, really hurting we can't help ourselves. We try to by saying, "My dad does stuff to me" or "Yeah, I do all kinds of drugs at the raves" or "My friend gets mad easily" or by letting the cuts we've made on ourselves visible to other people. We try to help ourselves but sometimes we can't because it feels as though fear of the unknown has us caged. So, because we can't pull ourselves up into the healing light, we can only hope that our friends will help us.

Once we, as friends, decide that the secret we've been told must be told, the next step is actually telling someone. Sometimes it's as easy as going to your school counsellor or youth minister, but sometimes we have to tell our parents the problem and let them take it from there. Our friends may become angry at first and may say things that they really don't mean. Some may even end the friendship but the real question that we need to ask ourselves is, "Would I rather lose the friendship or their life?" because if the secret involves self-harm, drugs, abuse or activity that we know is dangerous, then if it's not stopped, it will eventually take their life, or their spirit.

Think back at your highest moments: your highest highs, your greatest victories, your most daunting obstacles overcome. How many happened to you alone? Very few, right? When you understand that being connected to others is one of life's greatest joys, you realize that life's best comes when we invest in solid relationships. Of the people you know, who seem to enjoy life more in the negative, suspicious and anti-social? Hardly! The scrooges of life don't enjoy much of anything.

If you love God and people you'll find friends wherever you go.

And you'll get further in life too. John Luther says: ***"Natural talent, intelligence, a wonderful education; none of these guarantee success. Something else is needed: the sensitivity to understand what other people want and a willingness to give it to them. You don't win fame, recognition or advancement just because you think you deserve it. Someone else has to think so too."*** There is no substitute for a loving attitude when it comes to getting ahead.

People who alienate others have a hard time.
Here is why: *Significance of Friendship*

¾When others don't like you they try to hurt you
¾If they can hurt you they won't help you
¾If they are forced to help you, they'll hope you don't succeed
¾When they hope you don't succeed, life's victories are empty.

So, if you want more out of life, start investing in solid friendship!

Being a true friend, then, means putting their well-being above even the friendship because in the long run, it will save a life. Not only that but you will know that you cared enough about your friends to do something (talk) that was hard for you to do.

The Bible says that we are all brothers and sisters and we know that the ultimate act of love and friendship took place when Christ died on the cross for us. Likewise, today's friendships may require some sacrifice but in the long run, we won't have to live with regret and we'll have played a part in helping to show our friends the way back to health and happiness.

CHAPTER 20

THANKSGIVING: A PATHWAY TO LASTING SUCCESS

Thanksgiving is a necessary course for every winner. It is the path to a fulfilled destiny. It is a force that multiplies and increases. If you take the grace of God for granted you automatically get grounded. Until you appreciate God for where you are, He will not take you to where you are going. If you refuse to appreciate God for where you are you start to depreciate. Malachi 2:2 says;

> *If ye will not hear, and if ye will not lay it to heart, to give glory unto my name, saith the LORD of hosts, I will even send a curse upon you, and I will curse your blessings: yea, I have cursed them already, because ye do not lay it to heart.*

Be thankful, disappoint the devil. Someone said: "If you woke up this morning with more health than illness, you are more blessed than the millions who will not survive the week! If you have food in your refrigerator or store, clothes to wear, a roof over your head and a place to sleep, you are richer than 75% of this world! If you have money in the bank or in your wallet or handbag, you are among the top 8% of this world's wealthy! If you hold up your head with a smile on your face and truly thankful, you are blessed because the majority can, but most do not"! The lines above from the unknown author, though brief, speak volume:

2 Timothy 3:2 says:

Men shall be unthankful in the last days (Paraphrased).

We are living in an unthankful generation of millions of never satisfied children of a benevolent Creator. In 1 Thessalonians 5:18; the word reads: **"In all things give thanks"**. No matter where you find yourself, rejoice always and never forget that when there is life, there is hope. Even if you have no tangible reason to thank God for, you must daily lift up your voice and thank God for the gift of "LIFE". Do you know that thousands are dying as you are reading this book? Shame the devil! Thank God for your life today and declare the hope for the days ahead! One Zurich Proverb says": **"Optimism means expecting the best, but confidence means knowing how to handle the worst. Never make a move if you are** *Thanksgiving: A pathway to lasting success* merely **optimistic"**. Meister Eckhant wrote: **"If the only prayer you say in your whole life is 'thank you', that would suffice."** Laugh always! So that your life and endeavor can be called laugh Pavilion!

Making thanksgiving a life-style is the path to a lasting success. If you can't see the reason to thank God for where you are He won't see reason to bless you.

Fra Giovanni once wrote: **"Everything we call a trial, a sorrow, or a duty, believe me, the gift is there of an overshadowing presence."** Sometimes we must embrace pain and burn it as fuel for our life journey. Annie Baxter says: **"Something good always comes out of a failure"**. There is blessing in every burden, there is a story behind every glory. Nothing just happen, God will only permit and engineer the event and circumstances that will end uplifting you! Be thankful to God and shame the devil.

A story has it that many years ago in Central China, there was a farmer who used an old horse to plough his farmland. One afternoon, while working on the field, the horse dropped dead. Everyone was sorry and felt pity for him, but kept saying, **"Thank God we will see why"**. The community gave him a new horse to plough! Later in the year, the farmer's young boy went out riding on the horse and broke his left leg. Everyone in the village kept on saying "Oh what a misfortune again" but the farmer said, **"Thank God, we will see why"**. Two days later, without notice, the Chinese Red Army came into the village to draft new recruits. They forced many young people into the Army. When they saw that the farmer's son had a broken leg, they decided to leave him. After the Army departed, the villagers kept saying: "what a fortunate young man" but the old farmer then said: ***"Thank God now we see why"***. The boy's leg got healed weeks after. The truth was that this man always believed that God was in full control of whatever He allows into his life. If the old horse was not dead, of course, the boy would not dare climb on it and it may never have had a broken leg and may have been forced into the Chinese Red Army. In whatever situation you are in, refuse to complain; always remember Psalms 46:10. ***"Be still and know that I am God. I will be exalted in the earth"*** **St. Augustine said,** ***"Patience is the companion of wisdom"***. In any situation wait on God! Be still! You will soon know why and your praise and thanks will be the loudest.

If you continually acknowledge his doings in your life, you won't stop seeing His doings. If you don't thank Him for the little *Johnson. F. Odesola* you have today, you won't have much tomorrow. In as much as you might be far from where you are going, it is important to thank God for where you are.

Your being alive today is not by your power, it is God's grace that is keeping you, many who are more righteous than you are dead.

If you are disturbed about how some things in your life have turned always remember that with God as your controller and leader things will always turn out just right.

A boy once said to God, "You know what I want when I grow up". He then proceeded to give God his list: To live in a big house (A mansion), to marry a tall blue–eyed woman, to have three sons – one will be a senator, one a scientist and the other a footballer (sportsman). He also wanted to be a mountain climber and drive a red coupé (a sport car). As it turned out, the boy hurt his knees one day, while playing football. He could no longer climb trees, talk less of mountains. He ended up marrying a beautiful and kind woman who was short with brown eyes, instead of the blue eyes because of his business; he lived in an apartment in the city and usually rode the subway instead of a big house. He had three loving daughters instead of sons and they adopted a male fluffy cat. One daughter became a nurse, one an artist and the third a music teacher. One morning the man woke up and remembered his boyhood dreams.

He became extremely depressed. Heartbroken, he cried out to God: "Remember when I was a boy, I told you all the things I wanted:

Why didn't you give me those things? "I could have, said God, "but I wanted to make you happy" "Some of those things you asked for could have led you to your early grave."

Don't complain about your life. The Lord said in Jeremiah 29:11 that;

"For I know the plans I have for you", declared the Lord, plans to prosper you and not to harm you, plans to give you hope and a future.

Remember that when God modifies your plans, it is because He has the plan to make you a model for your generation. It is possible that you are far from fulfilling your goal and your boyhood vision didn't come to the way you intend it, but thank God you are alive, still fulfilling the plans and vision that God in His infinite wisdom has appointed for you. Suppose you are dead will you be thinking *Thanksgiving: A pathway to lasting success* and talking about fulfilling you goals. Keep hope alive, God is not through with you yet.

Before you think of not having enough shoes first thank God for your legs, if you don't leg have will you be thinking of shoes?

Before you think of not having enough food in your house thank God for divine health, suppose you are on hospital bed will you be thinking of food? You must acknowledge that health is greater than food. Before you think of the fact that you are delayed in getting marriage partner, thank God that you are a candidate of marriage, suppose you are blind or impotent will you be thinking of marriage There is no condition you are in that does not call for praise. If you can think well you will thank well. Celebrating what God has given you now, is the only way you can live the rest of your life in miracle. Determine to be thankful for what you have. Jeremiah 30:19 Says:

And out of them shall proceed thanksgiving and the voice of them that make merry: and I will multiply them, and they shall not be few; I will also glorify them, and they shall not be small.

Thanksgiving provokes multiplication! Praising provokes raising! If you are a thanks giver and a thanks liver, God will multiply you physically with good health. He will multiply you spiritually, God will multiply you financially and your joy, peace and rest will increase. In fact He will multiply your honour and subtract all indices of shame from your life and pursuit. The disgrace and disappointment of your enemy will multiply. If you praise God despite that delay and fire, you will not and cannot be few! You will multiply in due season, for God can not lie. When God measure men He does not put the tape around the head, but around the heart! So watch out of your heart!

There was a young lady who left the campus and began to follow all sorts of men thereby bringing so much dishonour, shame and disgrace to her parents. Her mother, who is a believer, instead of praising God for her daughter that at least she was still alive and walking with hope that God who captured Rahab was still on duty, was always weeping, complaining and bitter. But the more she complained the worse the girl became! Then one day she met a man of God who told her: "Won't you praise God for your daughter?" The mother angrily responded: "God forbid! How can I praise God for her disgraceful lifestyle? It was better she was dead!" The man *Johnson. F. Odesola* of God replied her "No you are not praising God for her evil ways you are giving thanks to God who gave you this daughter. You are giving thanks to God for helping you to nurse her to her young adult stage. Then you are to keep on thanking God in advance for the expected miracle of her salvation, no matter what you hear or see concerning her". At that point, the woman succumbed and began to sincerely praise God from that day. As she praised God daily, her own spirit broke out of discouragement and depression! Her heart became softened towards her daughter. Her faith in God rose like a legendary Phoenix and she experienced a miracle. The daughter suddenly came home at about 05:00am one day with profuse sobbing and tears in her eyes and asked for forgiveness from the mother. She said"; I was in a hotel last night with a man and suddenly it was like a veil was lifted from my eyes for the first time and I really felt naked and unclean. I felt I was a terrible sinner. I just got up, dressed up and began to return home." No matter how your life had been, no matter how delayed your expectation in life may seem, never listen to the melody of the devil; to dance into complaining. 1 Thessalonians 5:18 says;

In everything give thanks: for this is the will of God in Christ Jesus concerning you.

One Finish proverb says: *'He who does not look ahead remains behind".* Praising God in advance for that expected miracle is looking ahead! Do it daily and do it now while you are still reading this book.

Mathew Henry, the well-known commentator wrote the following in his diary. This was after they robbed him. "Let me be thankful first, because I was never robbed before; second, because although they took my wallet, they did not take my life; third, because although they took all, it was not much; and fourth, because it was I who was robbed, not I robbed". What a great thought from a great man of God!

Consider what God has done before, consider His greatness, consider His awesomeness and when you consider how He has delivered you in the past, and then let all these move you into the action of worship, praise and giving of thanks even in the present challenges.

Consider what God did 15 years ago! Consider what He did *Thanksgiving: A pathway to lasting success* within the last 10 years! Consider what he did 20 – 30years ago! Consider what he did for you or your loved one 50 years ago! Consider what He did for you while you were at school – from nursery to University education! Consider His pierced hand that has delivered you from trouble before. Do you know He can do it again?

Job 5:19 -20.

He shall deliver thee in six troubles: yea, in seven there shall no evil touch thee.

In famine he shall redeem thee from death: and in war from the power of the sword.

Samuel had an Ebenezer – a reference point of God's past goodness! You also set your Ebenezer for God's greatness and faithfulness to the intent that when the devil shoots arrows of defeat, discouragement and disappointment you scream back at him, "Behold my Ebenezer, Hither hath the Lord helped us"; The God who did it before will do it again".

Be positive about life and be thankful. The foundation for greatness is thanksgiving; if you miss it you miss all. Jesus gave thanks for the loaves and the two fish before five thousand people were fed and twelve baskets left over: Mathew 14:19 -21 says:

> *And he commanded the multitude to sit down on the grass, and took the five loaves, and the two fishes, and looking up to heaven, he blessed, and brake, and gave the loaves to his disciples, and the disciples to the multitude.*
>
> *And they did all eat, and were filled: and they took up of the fragments that remained twelve baskets full.*
>
> *And they that had eaten were about five thousand men, beside women and children.*

Thanksgiving has the power of multiplication. If you can genuinely thank God for where you are, everything around you will multiply automatically.

Choose to give thanks because all things work out together for your good future. Here is an excerpt expression of an unknown author titled **"Thank You Lord".** It goes thus:

"Thank you Lord for this sink of dirty dishes; It shows we have plenty of food to eat. *Johnson. F. Odesola*

Thank you for this pile of dirty laundry: it shows we have plenty of nice clothes to wear.

And I will like to thank you Lord for those unmade beds. I know that many have no bed to sleep on.

Thank Lord for slamming, screaming doors. It shows my kids are healthy and able to run and ply.

Lord, the presence of all these chores awaiting me shows that you have richly blessed my family. I shall do them cheerfully and I shall do them gratefully.

Thought I crutch my buckets and growl when the alarm rings; thank you Lord that I can hear. There are many who are deaf.

Though I keep my eyes closed against the morning light as long as possible, thank you Lord that I can see. There are many who are blind. Though I huddle in my bed and put off rising, thank you Lord that I have the strength to rise. There are many who are bed-ridden.Though the first hour of my morning is hectic when socks are lost; toast is burned; tempers are short and my children are so loud, thank you Lord for my family. There are many who are lonely.

Though our breakfast table does not look like the pictures in magazines and the menu is at times not balanced, thank you Lord, for the food we have; there are many who are hungry.

Though the routine of my job is often monotonous, thank you Lord for opportunity to work! There are many who are jobless.

Though I grumble and bemoan my fate from day to day and wish my circumstances were not so modest, thank you Lord for the gift of life; thank you lord"

What a powerful expression of thanksgiving.

Many go through life without thanksgiving God for the blessing that He has bestowed upon them. Remember to give thanks to the one who keeps and sustains you from day to day. He is our Shade from the "Sun" and the "Moon" of life (Psalms 121). He preserves you from the arrows that fly by day and the unseen arrows of the night. Thank Him for this: Praise and thank God for all the little things that we hardly ever think about. Where you have been is not half as important as where you are going. Keep hope *Thanksgiving: A pathway to lasting success* alive, if God has not been in control, things would have been worse. Many have been stagnated because of ingratitude, they cannot see what God has done in their lives and God cannot see reason to bless them. Get out of ingratitude; Praise God for where you are, acknowledge the grace of God in your life, then your destiny will be a reality. If you can thank God for your today, your tomorrow is secured.

CHAPTER 21

DOXOLOGY

Do you know this?

So, you may vaguely know that there might be God around, but you don't know much about him, who he is, whether he exists... Most people are quite content feeling this way, but is there any kind of meaning to life? Read on to find out. To illustrate my point, let me tell you a short story...

While on a hike in an area of marshy land, three men stumbled through some trees and then thought they could see something glinting, not far away. They figured that it could be something worth picking up, so they began to walk towards it. They could see it clearly now, a large silver coin lay on the ground a few metres away. As they approached, it suddenly shot away from them. Having, as most people do, about twice as much greed as common sense, they ran after it. After only a few metres, the ground felt slightly soft, but the men could see the coin so close now, that they didn't even feel it, - until it was too late. The first of the three put his foot down onto what should have been soft mud, and instead of being able to run on, he found himself floundering, waist- deep in muddy water, sinking further and further down. The second of the three tried to stop, but the third, as his view had been blocked by the second man, hadn't had time to stop, so they both fell into the quicksand as well.

Through the trees they heard a laugh: a laugh that was of pleasure at the men's misfortune... A boy walked out from between the trees, with coin dangling from a length of twine that was almost invisible. He watched them struggling in the marsh for a moment, then laughed again and ran off. The men were soon all shoulder- deep in the heavy sand; they couldn't get out, and were slowly sinking. They shouted, screamed... you name it, they tried every way of making noise there is.

Finally a young man dressed in a ranger's clothes ran over: as soon as he saw the men, he immediately began to pull them out. As he was helping to haul the last of the three out, he fell into the bog himself. The men of course tried to pull him out, but they couldn't: he was much shorter than them, and their floundering had made the "hole" in the quicksand much deeper. The young rescuer was Doxology quickly sucked beneath the surface of the mud. The men couldn't believe it: it should have been them in there; they didn't have a long life to look forward to like that young man! Why did it have to end up that way? He didn't deserve to die that way!

You may think that the story has a somewhat sad ending. True, it does, but what it illustrates does not. God's own son, Jesus, came down to earth and pulled us out of the quicksand. He died, was subjected to the worst kind of slow death imaginable because of us. He hadn't done anything wrong: he was perfect and blameless, and yet He died for us to pull us out of the quicksand of our greed and selfishness! He loves us so much that when He saw that we were doing wrong, He came and died for us, the whole of humanity, to save us.

God cares about you, he wants to be able to treat you as His "child". The reason Jesus had to die for us is because God can't have any kind of relationship with you if you have done anything wrong. When Jesus died He made it possible for us to ask God to forgive us for what we've done wrong, so that we can have a relationship with God. God's book, the Bible, tells us how we should behave, what is wrong and right and also gives a large amount of history from when the earth first came into existence, to a bit over 2000 years ago.

The Bible tells us that if we ask God to forgive us and obey what he has told us in the Bible then we will be able to live with Him in heaven forever when we die. Life with God is indescribable: He will help you and encourage you when you feel down, and he will show you what to do when you don't know. God is the most amazing person you could ever imagine.

Do you want to know God? Do you want a spiritual father who cares for you and loves you? If your answer is yes, then a good start would be to close your eyes, and say the following to him:

God, I know I've done wrong. I know I haven't lived the way you wanted. Please forgive me for all the wrong things I have done. Please help me to come to know you, help me to be able to trust you and obey you. Lord God, thank you for being my father, please be close to me now and always. **Selected**

BIBLIOGRAPHY

J. F. ODESOLA

'POWER for EXPLOITS'
Christ the Redeemer's Ministries P.M.B 1088
Ebute-Metta, Lagos Nigeria; 1997.

'RACING for EXCELLENCE'
Christ the Redeemer's Ministries P. M. B. 1088
Ebute-Metta, Lagos Nigeria; 1998.

'ON A MISSION TO THIS GENERATION'
Saviorite Nigeria Ltd
Lagos, Nigeria; 2006.

CANDIDATE FOR THE THRONE
Christ the Redeemer's Ministries P. M. B. 1088
Ebute-Metta, Lagos Nigeria; 1999.

SAM IGBARI

'TOO LOADED TO FAIL'
Agape Connection Publishing House
Ikeja, Lagos; 2002.

'THE LAWS OF UNCOMMON SUCCESS'
Agape Connection Publishing House
Ikeja, Lagos; 2003.

JEFF LUCAS

'GIDEON POWER FROM WEAKNESS'
Kingsway Publication
Eastbourne; 1999
THOMAS J. NEFF & JAMES M. CITRIN

'LESSONS from THE TOP'
Currency Doubleday Selected Bibliography

CHRIS E KWAKPOVWE

OUR DAILY MANNA Liberty Publishing House Lagos Nigeria; 2004

KIRK, A,
A NEW WORLD COMING,
London, Marshall's, 1983

WINTER, R D & HAWTHORNE, S C (EDS.),
PERSPECTIVES ON THE WORLD CHRISTIAN MOVEMENT: A
READER,
Carlisle, Paternoster Press, 1999.

JOURNALS:
MISSION STUDIES:
JOURNAL OF THE INTERNATIONAL ASSOCIATION FOR
MISSION STUDIES,
Hamburg, Volume IX – 2, 18, 1992.

INTERNATIONAL BULLETIN:
INTERNATIONAL BULLETIN OF MISSIONARY RESEARCH,
New Jersey, Volume 18, No. 3, July 1994.
**OTHER BOOKS BY THE
SAME AUTHOR**

*Advancing in Your call Exemplary Life of a Disciple Fishing for
Fruitfulness Walking in Dominion Telephone to Glory
Power for Exploits Candidate for the Throne Racing for Excellence*